THE PROMISE OF THE FUTURE:

A Financial Advisor's Guide to Effective Marketing

Duncan MacPherson

SUCCESS SOURCE
INTERNATIONAL

OTTAWA, CANADA

To Shawni

Acknowledgments

As with most meaningful projects, producing this book could not have been possible without the help of several good people. My three associates, who essentially run our consulting firm, Duncan MacPherson and Associates, Inc., made substantial contributions, ensuring that what you are about to read will be considerably more informative and enjoyable. Susan Rothery was assigned the job of editor, but her role went far beyond that. She made several valuable observations and provided countless suggestions, all of which led to a far more refined transcript. Terry Gronbeck-Jones has long been the engine of the company. He is an endless source of razor-sharp wit and wisdom, from which I have often drawn. Dennis Moseley-Williams has provided a bounty of diverse humour and profound insight. Thanks to the three of you. You have had a tremendous impact on this book, as well as on me.

I would also like to thank "The Big 3" of the personal development field whose ideas have meant a great deal to me. Few people can "axiomatize" the way Jim Rohn can. I have borrowed several of his thought-provoking principles, not only because they have affected me deeply but also because there isn't any better way to say them. His philosophy has left an indelible impression on me and inspired the title of this book.

Millions of people, myself included, have profited by having Brian Tracy as a "virtual mentor" by way of his seminars, cassettes and books. He is without question the hardest working person in the personal and business development field and has been an instrumental figure in the Learning Revolution.

Zig Ziglar is the consummate personal development "guru." So many people I've spoken with trace the turning point in their lives to Zig. He is a trailblazer and one of the most respected people in the field.

No one can translate a concept onto canvas better than Nick Gaetano. I couldn't have hoped for an image as powerful as that which he created for the cover of this book.

There are countless others whose ideas, codes of conduct and views of the world can be found in this book. A personal thanks is long overdue and I look forward to doing so.

A big thanks to my parents for having known when I needed steering in the right direction and when I needed to find things out for myself. Your judgment has made all the difference.

To Splinter for your unwavering loyalty. You were such a great sounding board during our early morning walks, and you always agreed with my ideas with an enthusiastic bark.

Saving the best for the last, to my wonderful wife, Shawni. You are my best friend and so much more. You have introduced me to all of the benefits of balance and perspective. You're the best.

Contents

Introduction

Even today, as I look back, I am still amazed at how this book came together. Frankly, it was a complete fluke. Without reminiscing too much, let me quickly review its evolution. Hopefully, you'll find it interesting.

Back in 1989, a friend and I were working for a successful electronics firm. Business was going well, and we both enjoyed reasonable success. Over time, however, we started becoming disillusioned with the direction the company was taking and as a result, we decided to build our own dreams and become entrepreneurs. The only problem was that we had no idea what we were going to do or sell.

So like all fledgling entrepreneurs, we headed down to Barbados for a month in order to put together a business plan. I think we discussed business ideas for all of thirty seconds. Fortunately, I had picked up a copy of *Success* magazine at the airport. We began to flip through it.

Toward the back, I found a small classified advertisement for a company that offered franchises in a specific region for anyone interested in selling personal and business development audiocassettes to business people. The reason the ad had caught my eye was that renowned motivational presenter, Zig Ziglar, was one of the names in the company's stable of speakers. (My father had given me a copy of Ziglar's book *See You at the Top* for my eighteenth birthday, and to say that it had made a profound impact on me would be a tremendous understatement.) As a result, when we returned home from the Caribbean I ordered a demo kit from the company. After it arrived, I listened to the cassettes diligently.

And then it happened. One of the cassettes featured a speaker by the name of Jim Rohn, a man whom, until then, I had never heard of. Without wanting to sound too dramatic, that little tape changed my life. I listened to it over and over and over again, to the point where I literally wore it out. The insights Jim passed along were like a splash of cold water. I still have the notes I took from my first listening experience, and they truly are among my most cherished possessions.

To shorten a long story, I asked my partner, "Why don't we promote the speakers rather than their cassettes?" Not only was I sure that it would be profitable, but I also reasoned that we would be able to attend all the seminars as well.

So off we went. Early on, we were quite lucky. Our first big event featured Zig Ziglar himself, and Zig's son Tom showed us the ropes, helping us to promote and orchestrate a very successful affair. In fact, we were so successful that we decided to repeat it, only this time with a twist. We had discovered that the people attending the first event were, ironically, the kind of people who needed the message the least

– they were very high-calibre individuals. Therefore, we decided to seek out a couple of companies to sponsor our next event in order to underwrite the costs and give it a little prestige.

The first firm we approached was a financial planning company. Our pitch was simple. We asked that they pay us a chunk of money and in return, we would hoist their banner on a wall, put their logo on the workbooks and give them tickets to dispose of as they wished. Not only that, we would conduct a VIP session for their best clients, let someone from the company introduce the speaker and provide a list of the attendees in order for the company to follow up and attempt to sell their services.

They jumped at the opportunity, and everyone walked away happy. The company was excited by the exposure they received and by the fact that it was hands-off, meaning that we did all the work. They were even more pleased by how much business they were able to generate, not to mention how strongly they fortified their existing client relationships.

Building from that success, my partner and I used the sponsorship framework as a prototype for future events, and we enjoyed good results. We promoted many of the most respected speakers and business trainers in the world. Not only were these people easy to promote and work with but each also had a distinctive message and style that left a lasting impression on me. It was win-win all around.

As the years went by, however, we began to encounter some rough spots with our big seminars. Without question, we hit a few home runs from our sales of tickets, sponsorships and back-end products such as tapes and books. Our problem was that with events this large, overhead was huge. When we made money, we made big money. But we also promoted a few events that flopped, and when they did, we *lost* a lot of money.

My partner became disenchanted, not only with the risk but also with the fact that the business itself was anticlimactic. Such is the life of a promoter. For example, we could spend weeks ramping up for an event, only to see it be over in a weekend. Come Monday, it was back to square one. We couldn't help feeling that we weren't really building anything. As he put it, we were trading our time for money, building only our speakers' dreams and not our own. So he decided to pursue another opportunity. He moved on, building a new business in a completely unrelated field, and today he is doing quite well for himself. As for me, I decided to hang in there. And then the next breakthrough happened.

It came about during a conversation with an acquaintance in the financial services field. "Duncan," he said, "if you want to make some real money, get into the business of money." He knew I loved marketing, and he suggested that I study the financial services field in order to help financial advisors create their own marketing plans. He added that he personally knew several advisors who were successful, but they were also flying by the seats of their pants.

Since many of my clients from the seminar days were financial advisors, I launched a fact-finding campaign to learn what it was exactly that made their businesses tick. My goal was simple: to discover what factors separated the best from the rest. I had a reason for needing to know. I had once observed two advisors, both of whom had started with the same firm at the same time, selling the same products and services in the same city. There truly wasn't much between them that varied. Yet three years later, one was excelling, making ten times the money of the other advisor. This situation fascinated me. What was it that had separated those two advisors?

I quickly learned that the difference was due to a principle called The Winning Edge. This concept simply suggests that while the disparities in rewards between the best and the rest are huge, the disparities in actual ability are quite small. And this situation applies to any field of endeavour. For instance, I spoke to an Olympic champion swimmer who trained three to four hours virtually every day for sixteen years and won the gold medal by three one-hundredths of a second. He told me that his rewards were ten times greater than those of the silver medalist, even though that he was not ten times better. He further told me that to get an idea of what three one-hundredths of a second looked like, I should pay attention to the amount of nail I removed the next time I trimmed my fingernails. That, he said, is three one-hundredths of a second.

Here's another example. A professional golfer wins the U.S. Open golf tournament and pockets four hundred and sixty-five thousand dollars for his efforts. He scores a four-round total of 276, meaning he averages sixty-nine strokes per round. If you do the math, he made close to seventeen hundred dollars every time he hit the golf ball. Down the leader board to the middle of the pack, you find another golfer who earns forty-six thousand dollars – ten times less than the winner. Was the winner ten times better? No. The also-ran, for lack of a better term, carded a four-round total of 284 for a per-round average of seventy-one. Again, doing the math, this golfer made one hundred and sixty dollars per shot, which still isn't bad. My point is this: the winner out-scored the average player by only two strokes per round, yet he made ten times more.

I learned very quickly that an advisor who earns ten times more than another advisor is not ten times better. He or she isn't ten times smarter or working ten times harder nor even spending ten times more on marketing. Basically, these advisors have attained that winning edge.

To get back to my story, I began to gather considerable momentum as a consultant to financial advisors. In time, my phone really started to ring with more frequency. Soon, after building a name for myself as a consultant, various financial services companies began asking me to speak at their sales conferences. I don't mind telling you how intimidating that experience was early on. I never considered myself to be a seminar speaker, and I got off to a rocky start. In fact, what I experienced in the first couple of months almost scared me away from ever speaking again.

On one memorable occasion, five minutes before speaking to several hundred people in the salon of a large hotel, I headed for the restroom to get focused. As I turned on the tap to wash my hands, water came gushing out like a fire hose, splashing the front of my taupe-colored pants. I looked at myself in the mirror, realizing, to my horror, what appeared to be an accident of another kind. I turned on the hand dryer in a frantic attempt to dry my pants. At that moment, I was sure my days as a speaker would come to a crashing halt. Fortunately, and with only minutes to spare, I dried my pants and delivered the seminar. On another occasion, after giving an afternoon seminar, I had to drive across town for an evening presentation. I was in the heart of downtown Toronto, trying to beat the street traffic at rush hour to make it onto the highway. Less than a hundred yards from the on-ramp, the transmission dropped right out of my car. Needless to say, I missed the seminar, and again reconciled myself to the thought that my career as a speaker was doomed.

Fortunately, I survived. I now travel around the world, delivering advanced marketing seminars for professionals in the financial services field. I'm not telling you this to impress you but rather to impress upon you the following simple point: my travels and my relationships with clients keep me closely in tune with *your* business.

What does that really mean to you? It means that none of these ideas are on trial. They have all been proven to work. This book is not filled with marketing theories. I didn't hide away in a cave, read a bunch of books on marketing and emerge a so-called guru. Yes, I have made a refined study of marketing strategies. But the success of these ideas came from my clients. I have learned far more from the advisors who have retained the services of our firm than they have learned from me. You've heard of 'Other People's Money' or OPM? Well, this book revolves around 'Other People's Experience' or OPE. We'll look at what to do and what not to do, both of which are worthy of study.

Every technique I recommend respects human nature. No matter how things change and how much technology creeps into our lives, human nature will always stay the same. Anyone who tailors their marketing approach to human nature will be in good shape.

That said, I'm not sure where I've caught you in your journey. You might be a novice advisor, looking to hit your stride or perhaps accelerate your progress. Or you might be an established advisor who wants to tighten things up and take your business to the next level. Chances are that you're doing a lot of things correctly right now. You might already have two of the three numbers dialed on the combination, and you just need the third number to realize a breakthrough. No matter what your circumstances are, I'm confident that you are going to find a few ideas that you can see yourself implementing. (It's interesting. Two people can hear the same idea yet have completely different responses. One might say, "This is great. This idea is going to blast my business to the next level," while another advisor responds, "Yeah, yeah, big deal. I've heard this stuff before." That's fascinating.)

That brings me to an important point. While there are literally hundreds of ideas in this book, ideas, quite frankly, are not the problem. Ideas are a dime a dozen. It's the *execution* of ideas that is the real problem. Your job is to sift through all of these ideas and translate some of them into results. Results, after all, are how you get paid.

But let me temper your expectations at the same time. More than likely you have already heard these ideas and others before. I'll be the first to admit that they are not new. (They might be new to you, but they are certainly not new.) Everything you are about to read is based on common sense. The reason why it might prove helpful to be reacquainted with these ideas is because common sense isn't always common practice. It's possible that you have forgotten what you once knew, in which case you will want to put some of these ideas back to work again.

You might find yourself motivated but overwhelmed in terms of where to start. This will be a defining moment for you and here's why: I did not write this book simply to motivate you. While motivation is important, it won't accomplish much on its own. And the reason it won't is because motivation comes in waves. I've been to enough motivational seminars to know this syndrome. They would get me all fired up and afterwards have me running to my car as excited as I could be. The problem was, by the time I got to my car, I couldn't remember why I was running. That feeling of motivation had already started to diminish. It had the enduring effects of a caffeine rush or a warm bath, full of impact but very short-term. That is because motivation is only one of the three key ingredients in the all-important equation.

The first ingredient in that equation is knowledge. If I want to build my business, I must first build myself. Knowledge alone, however, is not sufficient. Knowledge not invested nor applied is knowledge squandered. Which is where motivation comes in. However, in order to sustain the application, one must possess the final ingredient, self-discipline.

Tremendous results can be achieved with those three ingredients. Yet interestingly, while those three ingredients are available to all advisors, it seems that only a select few choose to constantly apply them. It reminds me of something I once heard Jim Rohn say. "The winds of opportunity blow the same for everyone; the difference is in the set of the sail." Hopefully, this book will help you to set the sail in a way that harnesses more of the wind.

As you go through the pages, I'm going to suggest that you consider what is called the ICE principle. This simply means that when you come across an idea that really hits home, making such sense that you want to apply it right away, highlight the idea and put an 'I' (for 'Immediately') beside it. If you come across an idea that makes sense but can wait for a while, write 'C' (for 'Consider') beside it. The 'E' stands for 'Eventually,' meaning that you like the idea, but it's unlikely you'll do anything with it until some point in the distant future. When you have finished reading the book, flip back through it and find the "I" highlights. Use them to put your marketing plan together.

The reason we use the ICE acronym is because I don't want you to become a victim of The Law of Diminishing Intent. It's the rule that says, "The longer it takes me to get around to doing something, the less likely it is that I'll do it." Get those ideas working for you right away. Experience tells me they will serve you well.

Duncan MacPherson
Ottawa, August 1998

Chapter 1

Marketing to Your Clients

Marketing to Your Clients

Tapping Into Your Greatest Asset

You might be asking yourself why I would start this book on the topic of client marketing. The reason is quite simple. For all financial advisors, existing clients are their most valuable assets. Yet often that asset is the most neglected form of business development and new client acquisition.

Here's how I know this: Most of our clients, financial advisors who hire us to create and implement marketing plans, have between three hundred and five hundred clients. (Don't let my numbers throw you. It doesn't matter how many clients you have.) That client base is referred to as an 'inner circle,' and it represents your most valuable marketing opportunity. Why? First of all, because of what is called The Rule of 52.

This rule suggests that every client in your inner circle has their own inner circle of at least fifty-two friends, family members and business associates. My contention is that your clients are not an end but a means to an end. They truly are a springboard to tremendous opportunities. If you examine the prospect hierarchy, your clients' friends and family members are among your best prospects. Your clients, however, will have far more persuasive impact on their acquaintances than you ever will. With that in mind, one of your most important goals is, in essence, to transform your clients into a sales force that will fan out across the countryside, waving your flag. In short, when your clients have a conversation with someone and the topic of money comes up, it should be a knee-jerk reaction that your clients brag about you.

The best way I can describe the importance of an inner circle is to introduce you to a marketing concept known as The Loyalty Ladder. This ladder consists of five rungs, and everyone in the marketplace is categorized as being on one of the five rungs. In ascending order, the rungs represent *suspects, prospects, customers, clients* and *advocates*. Throughout this book, we'll examine each category and what they mean to you as a financial advisor. As an overview, however, your objective regarding the Loyalty Ladder is to create what is called *conversion*. In other words, you want to convert people to move up the ladder from one rung to the next.

The bottom rung of the ladder represents people we call *suspects*. Frankly, a suspect is anyone with a pulse, anyone who can fog a mirror. Does it make sense that an advisor should spend his or her time and money on suspects? Obviously not. But I still see advisors everyday mistaking movement for achievement, meaning that they are very busy but busy talking to the wrong people. For purposes of illustration, let me give you an example.

An advisor once asked me for advice on a marketing initiative. He told me that he wanted to set up a booth at an upcoming financial fair. (At that point I thought, "*Financial* fair? Are there rides? Are there signs that warn, 'You must be this tall to invest'?") He explained that every year, a group of advisors organized this event. They covered the ice at his small hometown rink and set up tables to meet and greet people over a period of two days.

After a few minutes, I asked him, "Is this the best use of your time? I know that some trade shows are good events, but most of them only attract the trade show "junkies," those people who go to every trade show. They walk around with big plastic bags filled with hand-outs, and generally the bigger the plastic bag, the lower the calibre of prospect. Some of them are even professional about it. They arrive with their names on ink-stampers, seeking out and stamping every free-prize ballot in sight. So you are going to stand for two days with a goldfish bowl, asking folks to enter your draw for a free book, and hoping that you'll meet a few new clients, is that it?"

He gave me a weak smile and immediately started defending his position. "Duncan, hundreds of people are going to be there." At that point, I reminded him that it's more important to reach people who count than it is to count the number of people you're reaching. The question is, "Who?" not "How many?"

Reach the People Who Count
There is a big difference between a suspect and those on the next rung on the ladder – *prospects*. We are going to examine prospecting

5

in greater detail later on, but by way of an introduction, let me explain at this point that a prospect is someone who is predisposed.

'Predisposed' simply means that they are part of a methodically assembled geographic or demographic target market or that they have been referred to you by a client or promotional partner. Ultimately, a prospect is someone who calls you. It's an inbound call.

As you know, there are two types of phone calls: inbound and outbound. Inbound calls are when your phone rings with someone on the other end wishing to speak with you. Outbound calls are when you dial the phone, making it ring somewhere else. On that latter point, I am not a big fan of what is termed 'cold calling.' You aren't going to find much in the way of cold-calling strategies or role-playing scripts in this book. Don't get me wrong. I love the phone. But as you will soon discover, at the highest level of marketing, the telephone is a complement to your other marketing efforts. It is true that some people find cold calling productive and are pretty good at it. It is also true that you can cut down a tree with a hammer. It can be done, but there are other more efficient and less grueling ways to do the job. To be quite honest, I used to cold call in my business. I stopped when I met people who had never made a cold call in their lives yet had still gone on to build incredible businesses. As one of my clients once told me, "I only want the kind of people who slam down the phone when they get cold called."

Make Your Phone Ring

As an alternative to cold calling then, I ask that you consider the strategies in the Prospecting Section of this book that teach you how to make your phone ring. They are called *direct response* or *magnetic marketing*, both of which revolve around the Law of Attraction. Wouldn't it be great if you had a steady stream of inbound calls from prospects in response to your direct-mail campaigns? Wouldn't it be great if, after you worked a trade show or conducted a seminar, the key prospects called you the next morning? Some people think that it is a fantasy, but it's not. It's happening right now.

Savvy marketers understand that they are not trying to *create* prospects. They are trying to *find* them. It's like mining for gold. You have to move a ton of dirt to find an ounce of gold. You are not an alchemist, trying to turn dirt into precious ore. You have to sift good prospects from the mass of suspects, and you have to give them a reason to call you. But you can't want it more than they do. We'll examine later the qualities of a good prospect as it applies to your situation and how you can move that person up to the next rung on the ladder.

Once you've selected your prospects, you will want to convert them into being at the very least *customers*, those on the third rung. Why do I say "at the very least"? Because there is a big difference between a customer and those on the next rung of the ladder, *clients*. A customer is someone who has a hundred thousand dollars worth of assets with you but also two hundred thousand down the road with a competitor. Or someone else is providing your customer with a service because your customer doesn't realize that you offer that same service. A client, on the other hand, is someone who is exclusive to you. Every financial service you could possibly offer them is provided by you. Which brings me to the first reason that I'm so emphatic about client marketing. One of my favorite questions to ask a financial advisor is, "How many of your clients are exclusively your clients, versus how many of them are just customers?" Often the eyes of the advisor in question will glaze over like those of a deer caught in headlights when I ask this question. They have no idea.

Customers and Clients Are Great Prospects
I've found that most financial advisors have a lot of customers. As a result, there is a tremendous opportunity to uncover assets those customers might be holding elsewhere, to squeeze more juice out of the orange, so to speak, and to convert them into becoming clients. In other words, their customers are actually among their best prospects. It amazes me that in talking with advisors who have several hundred customers, I learn that rather than marketing to them, they focus on pure prospecting. I think they do this is because there is such an emphasis on new client acquisition and asset gathering. Personally, I believe it is too abstract to base your progress on the size of your book, the number of your clients or even your income. Instead, I think it's important to focus on your *yield* per client and yield per customer. Just as a farmer focuses on yield per acre of land, you

might be able to harvest business that is lying untapped within your existing client and customer base. In other words, you could be sitting on acres of untapped diamonds.

(For ease of description, all client and customer marketing efforts described from this point forward will simply be covered with the catchphrase 'client marketing.' What applies for one category, in terms of your marketing efforts, applies to the other.)

Work With People Who Are Already Convinced

To grow any business, you must either increase the number of customers you have, increase their buying frequency and/or purchase size, or increase the calibre of your client base. For some advisors, their existing clients can help in all three of these areas. There is a fulfillment issue involved as well. What would you rather do, spend your time convincing people or invest your time working with the people who are already convinced? It pretty much goes without saying which activity will be more rewarding.

Which brings me to the most important rung on the Loyalty Ladder and perhaps the most important distinction you can ever make as it relates to taking your business to the next level. It is where the real breakthroughs happen in marketing. The most meaningful rewards in this business go to the advisors who invest their time and money converting their clients to the top of the ladder, a rung reserved for *advocates*. A friend of mine refers to them as 'ambassadors.' These are the people who think you walk on water. They brag about you to the people in their inner circles. I'm sure, as you're reading this, you are thinking of some of your own advocates. Let me ask you this: based on the Rule of 52, what would happen to your business if you had one hundred advocates? Your business would be nothing short of amazing.

If you buy into the fact that clients are not an end but rather a means to an end, then you already know that the real value of a client is not in the commission you make but rather in the relationship you build with that person. The commission is undeniably important, but the client's commitment to you is worth even more. Why? Because a relationship lasts long after you've spent the commission. If you only focus on transactions, then you are trading your time for money, and we both know that is not a good trade. Clients who are loyal to you, who empower you with all of their assets and who endorse you to friends are truly what you are striving to achieve.

Allow me to explain this another way. A few years ago, I read a book called *The E-Myth* by Michael Gerber, which I highly recommend to all entrepreneurs. The premise of the book is simple. According to Gerber, all aspects of an entrepreneurial enterprise should evolve into systems. An entrepreneur should work *on* his or her business, not *in* it, in order to develop bulletproof systems. These systems increase efficiency and ensure that the business is not solely reliant upon the entrepreneur. Every system can become a prototype for duplication, enabling the entrepreneur to put the system into the hands of subordinates, thereby freeing time for the entrepreneur to focus on other, more productive activities.

Build A Sales Force

As an entrepreneur you too must think in terms of duplication. Of all the things you can duplicate, clients who endorse you are the most valuable. With every advocate you create, you are really hiring another sales rep who will be out there in the marketplace, stirring the pot for you. Your business will become more diversified and less vulnerable because it isn't reliant on one revenue generator.

I can tell if an advisor is doing a good job in the advocate department. I ask that person to tell me the percentage of new clients that are referred by existing clients. The minimum should be eighty percent. If you find that you are getting less than eighty percent of your new clients by way of referrals, then chances are you're leaving too much money on the table and frankly, you might be targeting your efforts in the wrong direction. This is fact, not speculation. And I'm emphatic about it because our best clients get one hundred percent of new clients referred to them from existing clients and promotional partners such as accountants, lawyers and the like (many of whom are the advisor's clients as well). These advisors have surely graduated from pure prospecting. They spend no time or money trying to convince new people. Every marketing dollar and every available minute is invested with people who are already convinced and are able to do the convincing. These advisors realize that it costs as much as five times more time and money to bring on a new client than it does to create a referral. Nothing is more persuasive than a third-party endorsement, and nothing is more rewarding than picking up the phone and speaking to someone who has been referred to you. The reach your clients have and the impact they can have on others is amazing. It's even more amazing when you consider whom they might impact. Chances are you have clients who know some pretty interesting people. If you ever need reminding, watch the film *Six Degrees of Separation*.

And it doesn't stop there. You'll remember that I talked about not trading your time for money. It truly is anticlimactic if you only focus on new client acquisition because you only get one benefit – a new client. When you market to your existing clients, you are actually multi-tasking. It's referred to as 'ensuring continuing results.' Like throwing a rock in a pond that splashes and creates a series of ripples, you will achieve three key benefits: uncovering assets, generating referrals and insulating your clients from competitive influences (or what I call 'competitor proofing').

Play For Keeps – Build A Wall Around Your Clients
If you have three hundred clients, any number of them are being hit on by your competitors as you read this. You therefore have to build a wall around them and instill in them a philosophy that says, "I

wouldn't dream of switching advisors; it wouldn't even occur to me." You have to anticipate client attrition and guard against it.

Part of your preparation involves reconstructing your attitude so that you don't delude yourself into thinking that everything is okay when in fact things are could be shaky. An excellent book that touches on this topic is *Only the Paranoid Survive* by Andy Grove, one of the founders of Intel. In it, he describes the positive benefit that comes from negative thinking. My interpretation of what he says is that you can't always believe your own hype.

Jim Rohn also expresses it persuasively. He compares business to the seasons. When things are going well, you are enjoying the autumn harvest. However, winter inevitably follows, and you have to ensure that you are well-positioned when it arrives. I use this philosophy because I've met advisors who feel that business will be terrific forever. Now, I'm not necessarily referring to doom and gloom. But it's naïve to think that you are immune to the natural ebb and flow of capitalism. As auto magnate George Romney stated back at the turn of the twentieth century, "There is nothing more vulnerable than entrenched success." Insulate your business from things out of your control and prepare for the unexpected. Confucius said it best: "Dig your well before you are thirsty."

With all of this in mind, let's take a detailed look at strategies I've seen advisors use successfully to create loyal, exclusive and referral generating relationships.

First, however, I'd like you to consider an important question: Do you have the ability and infrastructure to *grow* your business? Most advisors grow their businesses by attracting new clients. For others, it's not quite so simple. They already have a sufficient number of clients, too many actually. Some advisors have clients who are actually costing more than they are bringing, and the only way for these advisors to grow their businesses is through some form of voluntary attrition.

If you are like most advisors, eighty percent of your revenue stems from twenty percent of your clients, and twenty percent of your revenue stems from eighty percent of your clients. (This is the 80/20 Rule or, more specifically, the Pareto Principle, named for the early twentieth century economist.) In keeping with the notion of converting clients into advocates, do you treat the twenty percent that make up the engine of your business any differently than the remaining eighty percent?

Take a clue from the rest of the marketing world. After diligently researching their revenue sources, Saks Fifth Avenue, the exclusive retail store in New York, realized that a full fifty percent of its business came from the top ten percent of its clientele. Armed with this information, the store rolled out its exclusive Saks Club, which offers special incentives to top clients, such as private sales, sneak previews prior to new product launches and other benefits. As you can imagine, this program has further enabled Saks to fortify and enhance relationships with its most lucrative clients and stimulate more sales.

More and more, companies are taking extra care of their high-yield clients. Airlines create loyalty programs and offer special perks for their most frequent flyers. Hotels offer special upgrades and other perks to guests who stay at their facilities. I'm asking you, therefore, to take a look at what you do for your top twenty percent of clientele.

Service The Engine That Drives Your Business

The value of examining the energy one expends on favoured clients really hit home with a client of ours recently. He had booked a high-calibre speaker to give an evening presentation to his clients, all five hundred of them. We encouraged the advisor to hold a small VIP session an hour prior to the main event for fifty of his best clients, their spouses and a friend whom they felt might enjoy attending. The speaker agreed to hold a fireside chat, and the advisor arranged for the hotel to provide a nice selection of wines and cheeses. When the dust had settled, the advisor had generated more than twice the business from the VIP event, which had been attended by no more than eighty people, than from the main event, which had been attended by well over three hundred. Why? Because of who had been in the room.

I've said it once and I'll say it again: it is far more important to reach people who count than it is to count the number of people you are reaching. It truly is quite common for advisors to become so fixed on new client acquisition that they forget to think for a moment about the calibre of clients they are acquiring. I am absolutely convinced that you should create an ideal client profile and a MVP – Most Valued Prospect – profile. Chances are that the new clients you are looking to attract are exactly like your best existing clients. What is really interesting is that your best clients live near, work with, socialize with and refer people pretty much like themselves. This phenomenon is known as the Law of Environment, and it sees your best clients endorsing you to people just like themselves.

But it goes beyond that. The Law of Environment doesn't just affect what you get. It also affects what you become. You are a product of your own environment. The high-calibre clients that you attract bring out the best in you. Just as if you were to play tennis with a pro, by associating with top-quality people, you perform at your peak.

This philosophy is actually responsible for inspiring some advisors to disassociate from certain clients. We've had to help some advisors create an exit strategy because some of their clients were costing them more than they were making them. You and I both know that a client who gives you a couple of hundred dollars a month requires the same amount of time, lung capacity and output of energy as a client who gives you several thousand dollars a month. In fact, some advisors tell me that the higher-calibre clients are actually easier to service and have a lower hassle factor.

Holding VIP sessions for top clients or selling a portion of your book to another advisor are not signs of disrespect. Both courses of action are in your enlightened self-interest. You only have twenty-four hours in one day. We've helped advisors with eight hundred clients pare their client base. Granted, they had been making a ton of money, but they had no room to breathe. By reducing their client roster to less than three hundred individuals, in time they ended up making more money, enjoying themselves more and becoming more attractive to the marketplace. Before, they had been doing a disservice to the clients they had neglected – both those whom they had kept and those they had discontinued. In the end, everyone is now much better off. (You have to remember, "high road" or "true" success is achieved through the service of others. "Hollow" success is at the expense of others. Only strive to attract a number of clients that you can truly serve – no more.)

That said, I tell our clients to invest at least eighty percent of their marketing budgets in their clients. More specifically, I suggest that they invest 80% of that 80% into the top 20% percent, and invest 20% of the 80% in the remaining 80% of the client base. In essence, invest the most time and money with the people who most deserve it.

Where to Start
Now that we've established without question that your clients are

your most valuable assets, let's look at how we can transform your clients into fiercely loyal, referral-generating advocates.

We know that the marketplace does not reward those who need or want but rather those who earn and deserve. In keeping with some of most profound advice I have ever heard, you must start with an "earn the right" philosophy if you want to realize all the benefits that advocates provide.

What does it mean to *earn the right*? It means that you bring value to the marketplace, and in return, it rewards your efforts in abundance. The key is, if you want to bring value to someone that will have impact, you need to know what it is that person values. It never ceases to amaze me how little most financial advisors really know about their clients, let alone their prospects or promotional partners.

I first learned the value of data collection back in 1989 in an informative book by Harvey Mackay called *Swim with the Sharks Without Being Eaten Alive*. In it, Mackay described the Mackay 66, a sixty-six-point catalogue that he used to build a profile on each of his best prospects and clients. Designed to help him gather information, he used it to excellent advantage as relationships with all clients and network partners unfolded.

Today, I know financial advisors who know everything about their clients, right down to the names of their dogs. Nothing goes unnoticed; everything is stored in a client's profile. These advisors use a special contact management system (I personally use Maximizer™) and before they take a call from a client, they always bring the client's profile up on the computer screen. Details of each call are logged into the client profile so that each conversation can be invested in the next. I can't begin to tell you how well this process serves these advisors. On second thought, let me try.

A FORMula For Great Results

Once you've resigned yourself to the fact that you can't keep information of this importance stored in your memory, and once you graduate from notes on slips of paper in a client folder to a contact management system, you will need a framework with which to work. We encourage our clients to use a FORM campaign. In fact, it's not unusual for our clients to implement this campaign first as a foundation upon which other campaigns can be built. FORM is a simple acronym, suggesting that a solid relationship be built on four key pillars:

> F stands for Family
> O stands for Occupation
> R stands for Recreation
> M stands for Money

Most advisors usually have a good handle on the Money issues. What I'm asking you to consider is gathering as much information about Family, Occupation and Recreation issues as you do about Money. Here's why. The products and services you sell are your message. You are the messenger. What does a prospect connect with and buy first, the message or the messenger? The messenger. Why does a client leave a financial advisor and move his or her money to someone else? Is it because of the performance of the message or because of indifference with messenger? More often than not it's due to indifference.

However, most financial advisors promote the message instead of the messenger. This approach is flawed, especially in today's competitive marketplace. The message is not a unique selling proposition, meaning that it is not something exclusive to you. Moreover, if your client relationships never expand beyond profits, you'll rarely create advocates.

I am actually a case in point. I travel a lot and used to deal with the same travel agent for years. That is, until she moved to British Columbia. I no longer deal with the firm. She left and so did I. I was connected to the messenger, who just so happened to be selling a message.

Don't get me wrong. Making your clients a profit in and of itself is a great marketing tool. It's just not enough anymore. Ten years ago, all you had to do was make them money; today that is expected of you. As business guru Tom Peters will tell you, if all you do is meet your clients' expectations, you are vulnerable. Peters suggests that your objectives be in finding creative ways to stand out in the marketplace, in grabbing and holding people's attention and in being memorable. Meeting expectations is not memorable. Falling below or exceeding them is. Since I'm not a big proponent of falling below client expectations, let's focus on exceeding them.

Think back to the last twenty-minute conversation you had with your best client. How many minutes did you spend talking about money-related issues? More often than not, the better the relationship you have, the less time you spend talking about money. The rest of the conversation usually revolves around family, occupation and recreational topics. Or so it should.

Leave a Profit

Wouldn't it be great if all your client conversations were like those you have with your best client? It can happen if you'll focus not merely on making a profit but also on leaving a profit. When Jim Rohn first passed that piece of advice on to me, I thought 'profit' only related to money. He corrected me, telling me to think of the word's meaning in much broader terms. He said that everything I touched should be left better than when I found it. What a superb code of conduct by which to live!

Before examining ways to employ the FORM approach, let me dispel any skepticism you might have. It's not uncommon for a new advisor client of ours to resist this approach. Some advisors tell me that their clients don't care whether their advisors know anything unrelated to their financial goals. Fair enough. My response is, do you really want clients who won't let you get very close to them? These types of clients are far less likely to stay loyal to you, let alone give you all of their assets or referrals. Exceptions exist to every rule, but I've heard too many stories of advisors who make someone a thirty-two percent or fifty-four percent return, only to lose that person to a competitor.

Great relationships are as much a result of good chemistry as they are of solid credentials. The more you know about a client, the better equipped you are to demonstrate to that person that you care about his or her well-being. FORM information is the glue that fortifies your relationships. Friends don't fire friends; friends brag about them.

Some advisors find the process of gathering and storing FORM related information somewhat laborious. I suggest that they only gather and respond to FORM opportunities concerning the types of clients they want to duplicate or 'clone.' This might consist of only twenty percent of their inner circles. Secondly, I remind advisors of the importance of a marketing assistant to set up and drive systems that will support this initiative. Systems are essential. Henry Ford didn't invent the car and Ray Kroc didn't invent the hamburger. They invented precise systems that predictably executed the processes.

As far as gathering information, create a three or four page questionnaire and send it to clients. The response rate you realize from your clients is very telling. I can remember being invited into one office to help two advisors implement similar FORM campaigns. Both advisors had about four hundred clients. One advisor saw over seventy percent of his clients return the questionnaire on the first request. The other advisor had only a nine-percent response rate. The second advisor called me, saying the campaign had been a waste of time. My response was that the survey revealed the important fact that his clients were not well-connected and that he had some work to do. To me, the glass was half full.

I hope that this approach is consistent with your relationship-building philosophy. Before we examine how to get it working for you, I'll leave you with the words of novelist Bernard Malamud, who once wrote, "As you value the lives of others, yours achieves value."

Throwing Darts At Your Best Target

Let me show you how FORM and the 'earn the right' philosophy can help you build a wall around your clients and make them competitor-proof as well as uncover any assets they might be holding elsewhere and stimulate referrals. I've purposely chosen another easy-to-remember acronym which implies that your clients are your best target market: DART. (Did I mention that I really love acronyms?)

> D stands for Deserve
> A stands for Ask
> R stands for Reciprocate
> T stands for Thank

The Latin origin of the word 'deserve' stems from the words "to serve" or "from service." I am convinced that client service is among the most important marketing investments you can make. Client service is not a service expense. I've seen financial advisors use a conveyor-belt approach to bring on new clients only to have their efforts sabotaged by poor client service. You can have the smartest marketing plan in the world, consisting of the best marketing strategies money can buy, but clients will still fall through the cracks and migrate to competitors if client service is trivialized.

You won't find me preaching to you about infrastructure as it relates to service nor am I going to lecture you about personal conduct in a service-related situation. My goal is to pass along the benefits of great service as they relate to marketing.

There are two types of service, reactive and proactive. 'Reactive' service speaks for itself. It's when you respond to something that has occurred. Perhaps it's something bad that has happened, and you aren't even the one who caused it. 'Proactive' service is taking the bull by the horns, whether preemptively or after the fact. The Chinese word for "crisis" consists of two symbols, one meaning "problem", the other "opportunity." You take something negative and make it positive.

The Pendulum Swings

As an example, I can remember doing some seminars on the road on behalf of a good client. A representative from the firm volunteered to drive me from one event to the other rather than having me rent a car. Following the last seminar of the day, we drove to my hotel in a nearby city for the next day's seminar. To thank him for chauffeuring me, I decided to buy him a copy of a book that we had discussed in the car. I called a bookstore across the street and inquired if they had the book in stock. They did, so later that evening I headed over to buy it.

Upon arriving, I was disappointed to learn that the book wasn't there. While the clerk had seen it a day or two earlier and had assumed it was still on the shelf, it had in fact been sold. I decided to buy the book once I returned home and to mail it to the rep who had driven me.

It was at this point that the manager of the bookstore took action. She called a branch across town which had several of copies of the book on hand. Without a car, however, I couldn't drive over.

Rather than placing blame or making excuses, the manager took serious ownership of the problem and called her husband at home, asking that he drop by the branch and pick up a copy. You can imagine my amazement when, thirty minutes later, I had the book in my hand. Client service truly is a marketing expense; in the time I had waited for my book to arrive, I had purchased three others. Problems and mistakes really can lead to opportunities.

I Own This Problem!

Your response is critical, especially if you didn't commit the mistake. Clients don't care about the details of a problem, nor do they want to endure long-winded explanations. They just want the problem to go away. If a mutual fund company errs on a client's statement, or if a transfer gets forgotten, the client wants it fixed. The best thing you can tell a client is, "I own this problem. You won't hear from me until it is more than solved. That's why you hired me." Then set out to rectify it.

The message you need to communicate is that you don't take problems lightly. As with investment returns, service is expected. However, unlike investment returns, you're a hero when you exceed expectations.

Furthermore, don't wait for a problem to happen to demonstrate great service. Problem prevention is the ultimate goal. Be proactive.

I never tire of hearing about a company that understands the power of preemptive service. One of my favorite examples is that of Lee Valley Tools. Founder Leonard Lee, a true marketing visionary, recognized the demographic shifts occurring in the marketplace. He foresaw more baby boomers, with free time and disposable income, pursuing hobbies such as gardening and woodworking, and he opened a company to satisfy those needs. He also realized that gardeners and woodworkers tend to hang out with other gardeners and woodworkers. He decided that, rather than spend marketing money trying to convince new people by way of advertising, he would invest his marketing dollars with the people who were already onside as clients. In other words, his company would offer first-class proactive service.

If you were to buy a $16 hammer by mail order from Lee Valley Tools and two months later, it went on sale for twelve dollars, you would automatically receive in the mail a cheque for $4 with a letter explaining why. Let me ask you something. You are standing on your front porch, and you've just opened an envelope to find this cheque and letter. What are you saying to yourself? WOW! (That's just before you race to the phone to tell your woodworking buddies.)

Speaking of 'wow,' I recommend you read *The Pursuit of Wow!* by Tom Peters, whose corporate insights I have already alluded to in the preceding section. It is filled with stories of companies around the world that invest their marketing time and money by dazzling their existing clients.

Take Advantage Of Low Expectations
It all comes back to exceeding expectations. The reason why it is so powerful is because poor service has become so much the norm that average service stands out. Isn't that a sorry statement!

I fly a lot, and I'm a top-level member with several airlines. One of their client perks is to provide a special phone line where our calls are answered promptly. This is supposed to be a perk? To me, that's an admission of mediocrity. Promptness should be a given. My point is this: when you dazzle someone, make it memorable. Nothing pleases me more than businesses, whether they are enormous corporations the size of Disney or mom-and-pop stores on an urban street corner, that understand the long-term benefits of good service. It might not have an impact on your next paycheque, but it will have an impact.

As a financial advisor, one of the most efficient proactive service techniques available to you is a 90-Day Call Rotation. With this technique, you initiate a call to each of your clients at least once every ninety days. (Call rotations are independent of inbound client calls.) If you have four hundred clients, then you would be calling five or six of them each day. Reflecting on the Pareto Principle, you might want to do a 30-Day rotation for your top clients and have your assistant use the 90-Day rotation for the remaining eighty-percent. It's up to you. Just create a system and stick with it.

I say "system" because systems are far less fallible than people are. Advisors without systems have a tough time approaching tasks methodically rather than spasmodically. I fully realize that this approach is a fundamental technique. As Vince Lombardi once said, "The best in any field are simply brilliant at the basics." Staying on track and achieving your goals doesn't happen because of fancy strategies and esoteric tactics. True success is a result of a few simple disciplines practiced every day.

If it's as easy as that, why don't all advisors select and stick to the basics? Because basics are boring. Nor do they pay dividends right away. It's like investing. We both know that value investing (combined with a recipe of discipline, patience, dollar-cost averaging and so on) will eventually pay off. Yet its very lack of excitement and instant gratification drives some people to invest in areas which make for compelling conversation yet, on closer inspection, are deeply flawed.

Most advisors don't want to be told that they can achieve amazing success from simple approaches like call rotations. Most advisors want to hear about marketing ideas that have a little drama, a little pizzazz, things like fax broadcast systems, fancy audio business cassettes, sophisticated software programs that blanket a city, assisted by an army of cold callers following up. To those advisors, that's excitement!

Keep It Simple

At the risk of oversimplifying marketing, my advice is: Keep it simple. I'll admit that you can go through an entire month of call rotations and not generate a sniff of business. I also realize that I can rip out "M" in the white pages, start 'dialing for dollars' and stumble into a few customers instantly. But I come right back to multi-tasking. Remember, your goal is not just client acquisition. It's also competitor proofing, uncovering assets and generating referrals.

Call rotations lead you to that end. Give the process a chance to compound and to gather momentum. Make it a habit. Once it becomes habitual, the activity will take on a life of its own. According to Aristotle, "Quality is a habit, not an act. We are what we repeatedly do."

Nothing could be more important than habitually calling four or five clients each and every day. You don't have to be the bearer of profound news. Simply calling a client to say that you have been thinking about her and commenting on her daughter's ballet recital is pretty powerful. You can use technology to advantage as well. Several advisors have told me how leaving a voice-mail greeting or sending an e-mail message out of the blue has left a positive impression. (This takes away the transparency that comes with only calling when you are trying to sell something or during an urgent market-related event.)

How Am I Doing?

Another example of proactive service is best explained in the A, or Ask section, of our DART acronym. Anything you want your clients to do, ASK them. If you want to competitor-proof your clients, ask them how you are doing. Obviously, call rotations indirectly achieve this objective because they give clients an opportunity to raise an issue that might not be sitting well with them. You shouldn't rely on it exclusively, however, because it isn't always as revealing as you would like.

Usually in the summer we encourage our clients to rollout a client-survey campaign. It goes without saying that the best way to raise the bar is to ask the people who receive the service. Responses to the survey are both efficient and revealing. Think of the economies of scale. For all intents and purposes and in terms of time and money, your output costs don't vary much whether you send out ten surveys or two hundred. As I mentioned earlier with the FORM campaign, your response rate tells you how well-connected you are to your clients. Even for those clients who don't respond, the campaign has a positive impact: you are showing those clients your commitment to improvement. There really is no down side. For these people who respond, you can gain valuable feedback about how they feel about doing business with you. As the ancient phrase suggests, the truth shall set you free.

The campaign unfolds with a letter to clients. At the top of the letter is a quote such as, "A customer is the only critic whose opinion really counts," (Mark Twain) or, "If there is a better way to do something, find it," (Thomas Edison). The letter continues by stating the pride you take in offering your clients great service but that you never want to be satisfied since improvements can always be made. You request that the client fill out the questionnaire and send it back, providing a name only if he or she wishes.

Typical questionnaire items include:

- "What led you to select our team?"

- "Have we exceeded, met or fallen below your expectations?"

- "What needs to happen in the coming years for you to feel satisfied with our relationship?"

- "We are planning to offer new value-added services for our clients. Which of these would appeal to you (lending library, client lunch-and-learn sessions, website, etc.)?"

Asking For An Opinion Makes A Statement

The questions you select are ultimately up to you. Just be certain that you make the survey easy to complete and meaningful. Completed questionnaires also give you something to talk about during upcoming call rotations for both those who made suggestions and those who forgot to participate. Several advisors have also successfully melded their client surveys with FORM-related questions. The bottom line is that your clients should enjoy a sense of empowerment when asked for their opinions. Surveys can uncover many things that would never have been raised until it perhaps became too late. For example, one advisor, resistant to call rotations, sent out a survey to his clients. One of his top revenue-generating clients returned the questionnaire blank, save for the following comment at the bottom: "I'm thinking of moving my account. I never hear from you." The advisor was shocked. Today he is faithful to completing call rotations, and he still has that client onside.

An interesting by-product of this campaign is the acquisition of testimonial letters. Several advisors have sent thank-you letters to their clients once the survey has wrapped up. (Even those who didn't respond get the letter to validate the campaign and its results). For clients who sing the advisor's praises, the thank-you letter is customized to include a paragraph that gently requests a favour. The client is asked to authorize the advisor putting his or her questionnaire within a plasticized sheet in a binder at the office for prospective clients to peruse while in the waiting room. It's not uncommon for some of these clients to go so far as to write a formal testimonial letter to accompany the survey. The persuasive impact of this endorsement on a prospect is huge.

Another example of asking for feedback is by way of a Client Advisory Council. While I'll discuss this concept in more detail in the promotional partnering section, let me give you a quick snapshot. An advisor invites his or her top dozen business owner-clients to a nice lunch and round-table discussion. The advisor informs them that the purpose of the meeting is to brainstorm with valued clients about ways to refine his or her business.

Line Extensions

The asking doesn't stop with client service issues. If you want to uncover assets that your clients might be holding elsewhere, or if you want to introduce a new service to your clients that they might not know you offer, you need to ask. And you do that with a line extension campaign.

Large companies roll out line extension campaigns all the time. Snapple Beverages, for example, started eroding Coca-Cola's market share. To compete with Snapple, Coke introduced Fruitopia. They also introduced Powerade to compete with Gatorade and Barq's Root Beer to compete with both Dad's and A&W's root beer. Coke doesn't care which one you drink as long as you get it from them.

Besides using line extension campaigns to find money your clients have maturing elsewhere, they are used to inform clients of a service you offer that they are having fulfilled elsewhere. For example, you might have recently qualified to offer insurance products. Your clients, therefore, need to be informed. Remember that the more you have of a client's assets, the more insulated the client is from competitive influences.

An important distinction about asking your clients for more business is to be careful about *how* you ask. Do not bring them your needs. Your clients don't care about *your* needs; they care about *their* needs. This is why it is so important that every request you make be presented in such a way that your clients perceive it to be in their best interests. And an obvious caution with respect to line extensions is to be mindful of how many times you go to the well.

Experience tells me that there are two types of marketers in the financial services field, heroes and hucksters. I can identify a huckster in about ten seconds. When I read a letter that they have sent out to their clients, I can read between the lines the glaring message, "I need the money." Heroes, on the other hand, never compromise the integrity of their client relationships by sending an obvious marketing message with a needy theme. They always take the high road and err on the conservative side with subtlety and professionalism.

Rely On Imprinting And Social Proof

Imprinting is one of the most intriguing aspects of marketing. It occurs when several gentle reminders are used over a period of time to create a higher level of familiarity and interest rather than when using one big advertising splash. My favorite big-business imprinting company is Nike. Phil Knight, Nike's CEO, paid golfer Tiger Woods forty million dollars to wear the Nike swoosh for the next ten years. The logic behind this sponsorship is that if you see the Nike swoosh frequently enough, you will automatically buy Nike the next time you need sports clothing or equipment. Incidentally, the first year Nike had Tiger Woods onside, the company's sales of golf apparel doubled.

Marketing is a lot like investing. Occasionally, you hear of someone who made a lot of money in a quick hit, but more often you hear of the disappointments from people who took the fast route. Most people become wealthy by following simple time-tested strategies and by taking advantage of compound interest. Just remember that it isn't only money that compounds. Disciplines compound too. Imprinting may not impact your next paycheque, but it will compound and take on a life of it's own if you give it a chance. Nothing goes unnoticed; every imprint is an investment in the next.

Before we look at examples of imprinting, let me touch on the value of social proof marketing. Social proof is a compelling marketing tool because it comes from a third person's endorsement. Various critics frequently lace movie ads with favourable testimonials. Remember the advisor who kept a well-placed binder of social proof letters in his waiting area? There is an old marketing maxim that says, "Ducks walk to water in single file." In other words, they tend to follow others who take action first.

Social proof is non-threatening and particularly effective when used in line extension campaigns. (An imprinting campaign is a term used to describe several appeals to a client to act on an offer you have made.) Social proof tells your clients that the only reason you are marketing a new or forgotten service is because of questions, requests and interest from your other clients. That said, let's look at the ways and means of rolling out a line extension campaign.

Be Targeted

As with all marketing campaigns, before you launch one you must be well-targeted. Obviously, if you already know the details of a client's investment plan and if you have a good relationship with that person, then targeting is not an issue. But what about longtime clients whom you haven't spoken to recently? I strongly recommend you send them a client survey and/or FORM questionnaire, asking some leading questions to pique their interest and awareness. Questionnaires don't only reveal a client's level of satisfaction; they can also be quite telling about changes in your clients' financial situations.

Be sure to include the following types of questions in your client surveys and questionnaires:

- "There are several pieces to the financial puzzle. Have we done a good job educating you about (and list the services with a yes/no check box beside each)?"

- "To make informed financial decisions, we have a popular Asset Monitoring Process which allows us to help clients track the progress of all of their investments, including those held at other institutions. Would this be of interest to you?"

Keep Imprinting for Awareness

Keep reminding clients about other needs they might have. The 'PS' section at the bottom of your letters is often the most vividly read part, so use it to advantage. It's a great place for a call-to-action. For example:

- "Recently, a number of my clients have been inquiring about (issue). If you happen to have any questions about (issue) as well, please call me at your convenience, and we'll discuss a proper course of action."

As an aside, always ensure that your letters have a friendly, personalized tone. Every one of your clients wants to believe that he or she is your most important one.

Newsletters also play a strong role in building awareness about various products and services that you offer. You might, for example, create a "Did you know?" section in every issue where you highlight a product or service. "Did you know that your most valuable asset is not your house or your car?" Then continue on with a disability insurance feature. The "Did you know?" concept has proven to be intriguing. Remember the old American Express ads that started off by saying, "Do you know me?" They were very effective at grabbing people's attention.

The beauty of building awareness is that it gives you something else to point to and discuss in future call rotations. "By the way, a lot of people have had questions about the Disability Insurance spotlight I had in my last newsletter. Do you have any concerns?"

Another effective technique is a campaign called Post-Summer Reviews. Send a letter to your clients that states:

- "I hope you had a great summer. We haven't spoken for a while, so now would be a good time to get together, examine your progress and see if any minor adjustments need to be made. As you know, timely minor adjustments can lead to major improvements."

The letter invites the client to do the review either over the phone or in person, depending on the client's (and advisor's) preference. Some advisors meet with their clients' accountants, while others do a variation of this campaign for the day after a client's birthday. Whatever your approach, good things happen when you talk to or meet with your clients. It's certainly conducive to uncovering assets or discovering new needs based on clients' changing circumstances.

Client Chemistry

The phone and one-to-one meetings are still the most powerful ways to uncover business. The key to each one is the subtle, understated manner of your requests for new business, and the rapport you have established with each client. I'm convinced that even when it comes to time-sensitive issues, such as maturing investments, gentle reminders are all that are needed to attract new assets. I mentioned before that competitor-proofing, uncovering assets and stimulating referrals are as much about chemistry as they are about credentials.

I've spoken to a great number of advisors regarding their success at uncovering assets, and virtually none of them could tell me of specific techniques they used to achieve those ends. They are just 'good' people. Whether it's call rotations, clients' reviews or simple PS imprints in letters, uncovering assets is as much about consistent communication as it is nifty techniques. Interestingly, some advisors have told me that one condition of doing business with them is that they must manage all of a client's money. It's a bold approach and one we'll examine in more detail later.

Let's talk about asking for referrals. I'm convinced that the main reason clients don't refer their advisors isn't because they don't want to, but because it probably just hasn't occurred to them. Perhaps they feel the advisor is too busy and can't take on any new clients. I'm also convinced that the main reason financial advisors don't ask for referrals is because they fear rejection. Which brings us right back to imprinting. Our company's best clients – financial advisors who get 100% of their new clients referred to them – never ask for referrals. They are, however, very good at reminding their clients that they take referrals.

When we lay out marketing plans for established financial advisors, the plans usually consist of twelve 1-month or six 2-month campaigns. With each campaign, we select spots to subtly imprint a non-threatening reminder about referrals.

Start Them Off Right

When you bring on a new client, begin the imprinting process. At the end of "the signing ceremony" (as a friend of mine likes to call it), use what is called the "oh, by the way…" approach. Several advisors use a variation of this approach as they are winding down a meeting with a new client:

- "By the way, I have to tell you that one of the most fulfilling aspects of my job is helping people make informed decisions about their financial futures. As you know, financial success is a matter of choice, not chance and because everyone's financial situation is unique, it's not uncommon for my clients to ask me to answer questions for a friend or family member. If you know someone who has financial concerns, have that person call me. I'll make the time to answer their questions."

The "oh, by the way" is also known as The Columbo Close, named after the television detective played by Peter Falk in the 1970s. Used verbally or in letters, it can be very disarming.

The 'PS' is also a good place to plug a referral. For purposes of illustration, let's say you heavily emphasize estate planning. Your 'PS' at the bottom of a Post-Summer Review letter could read:

- "Oh, by the way, several of my clients have been referring their friends and family members with personal questions about estate planning. As you know, I pride myself in being an estate-planning authority. If you are speaking with someone who is concerned or simply needs a second opinion, have him or her call me. If they're a friend or family member, I'll make the time to answer their questions."

Another effective 'PS' is:

- "By the way, I would be remiss if I didn't take this opportunity to thank my clients for waving my flag to their friends and family members. As you know, my business has been built on word-of-mouth advertising, and it makes me feel great to know that you have the confidence in me to refer me. It is the highest compliment I've ever been paid. Thank you."

There are events that take place in the marketplace that are perfect for a subtle 'PS' referral imprint. Say, for example, that after a long period of strong market gains, a little volatility presents itself:

- "PS. By the way, in light of the recent stock market turbulence, a number of my clients have referred people with personal financial questions to me. It's no surprise some folks might be a little concerned and need a little reassuring. As always, I'd be happy to help out.

You can imprint for referrals in a client survey by asking, "Have we earned the right for you to feel compelled to refer us to a friend or family member?" Provide yes or no check boxes. Some financial advisors tell me that many of their best clients have answered that question by stating that they didn't realize the advisor was taking on new clients.

Your newsletter is a useful tool in this regard. Place a photo in which you are donating money to a worthy charity on behalf of your clients. The caption under the picture can read, "A small token of my appreciation on behalf of my clients who are forever referring friends and family members to me."

Pick Your Spots

The key is to pick your spots. Be subtle. One financial advisor told me that he basically plants seeds when he speaks to his clients on the phone. As each call unfolds, the client invariably asks the question, "How's business?" The advisor responds, "Business is booming. And it's funny, I was thinking about you the other day. A good client referred a business associate to me, and he reminded me of you. He too likes (insert interest)."

The bottom line is give the imprinting approach a chance. Temper your expectations; the compounding benefits will pay off. But don't forget to ask. A simple reminder is usually all it takes. Remember, people like to refer because it gives them a sense of empowerment. If they know you'll make them look good, they'll go to bat for you.

The Law Of Reciprocity

Let's now look at the R in DART, which stands for Reciprocate. As the ancient phrase goes, giving starts the receiving process. The Law of Reciprocity suggests that if you endorse others, you'll be endorsed. If you have ever referred business to a client, you already know the impact of this philosophy. Be obsessed with steering business to your clients. As you'll see in the promotional partnering section, few things are as powerful in fortifying relationships.

Here is how you can imprint the referral concept at the end of the signing ceremony with a business-owner client:

- "By the way, give me a bunch of your business cards. I meet a lot of people on a regular basis, and if I meet someone who can use your service, I'm going to give them one of your cards. Is that okay?"

That person won't say no, I can tell you that much. In fact, chances are you won't only get some cards but you'll be asked for a few of your own in return.

Incidentally, don't forget to patronize your clients' businesses when the opportunity presents itself. David Ogilvy, of the world famous advertising firm Ogilvy Mather, went out and bought a new Rolls Royce the day his firm was awarded the Rolls Royce account. (Let's hope that you don't ever have a client who sells restored Pintos. Yikes!)

Which brings us to the T in DART. It stands for Thank. You can't thank your clients enough. People like to be recognized and appreciated for their efforts. Everyday, people are bringing value to your life and your business. Are you taking the time to thank them?

New Client Welcome Process
Buying financial services can be an anticlimactic experience for your clients. Think about it: when they buy a new $50,000 car, they have a new car to show for it. When they buy a $300,000 house, they have a new house to show for it. When a client walks out of your office, what does he have to show after giving you three hundred thousand of his dollars for you to manage? A receipt? Maybe a business card?

When you buy a new house, a good realtor will deliver a house-warming gift once you move in, such as a welcome mat or brass mailbox. When you buy a new car, it's not uncommon for a good sales rep to give you a gift basket or to take a picture of you with your new car so that she can have it laminated and made into a calendar for you.

You can't tell me that what you sell isn't at least as important as those two purchases. You sell the promise of the future, and that's pretty abstract material. So I encourage you to make the abstract more tangible. We've helped countless advisors implement the following simple process:

Step 1: The Day of the Signing Ceremony

Before the door has even closed behind your client, write a personalized thank-you card. Do not mention business, as it will cheapen the meeting. Do not say, "Thanks for the business" because that essentially means, "Wow, the trailer fees on this transaction are going to be tremendous, thank you very much." Instead, connect on the messenger level. For example, you might write:

- "I really enjoyed our meeting today. It was good hearing about your son's hockey try-outs. I'm looking forward to a great relationship. Welcome aboard."

Step 2: One Week after the Signing Ceremony

Send a formal letter to your new client, thanking that person for selecting you. Mention that you don't take your responsibilities lightly and that you look forward to working together. Reiterate that you take a team approach to client service, and start the process of familiarizing your new client with your staff by detailing their roles and responsibilities.

Step 3: Two Weeks after the Signing Ceremony

Send a three-ring binder or attache with another letter that says:

- "We take great pride in helping our clients stay organized. We realize that you get bombarded with financial documents, so we are providing you with this handy system. Put your important documents inside and bring them with you to our annual reviews and other meetings."

Some advisors go all out and give their clients a $40 leather model. Others are more frugal and send a simple four-dollar binder with a printed cover insert. Others establish thresholds. For instance, if the client's assets are over $250,000.00, they would get the leather version; if not, they get leatherette. Regardless, I encourage that you include tabbed sections for statements, insurance, legal, taxes and other accounts. Also include a FORM questionnaire with instructions to complete and return it. You'll be amazed at how many assets these simple binders uncover down the road. When the client has to find a home for an inheritance or other money that has finally matured, more often than not the "go to" person will be the one who sent the binder.

Step 4: First Statement Review Call

Because your statement is different from those your new client received in the past, call to ask if he or she has any questions. Be certain everything is clearly explained and understood.

Which brings us to true value of this process. Your new clients have been dealing with other advisors for the last however many years. As a result, your new clients have certain expectations. This four-step process will validate in their minds that moving to you was the right thing to do.

For clients who came to you as a result of a referral by an accountant or another client, be aware that both will be talking about you sometime in the near future. By using this approach, you insure that your new client will tell the person who endorsed you, "The best thing I did was speak to your advisor…" The likelihood of future referrals just went up dramatically.

Referral Recognition

So your new client now thinks you're a star. But don't forget to do something for the person who endorsed you. When recognizing someone who sends you a referral, consider two things: impact and shelf life. For impact, send them something that catches them completely by surprise. You don't need to get into the gift-giving business nor do you need to spend a lot of money. It's more important that you be thoughtful than buy something expensive. For clients who referred you, the best guideline is to go right back to FORM. Send them something that you know relates to their family, occupational or recreational interests. What you send should stop them in their tracks and scream out, "I'm paying attention!"

Make It Last

Shelf life refers to the length of time the gift you send will last. If you send the person who referred you a gift certificate for a restaurant — even if it's one you know they like — the impact is good but the shelf life is not.

(As a funny aside, I once referred a friend to another friend in the leasing business. The leasing friend knew I played golf, so he sent me a box of golf balls. I called him back and said, "Nice impact, lousy shelf life." Because if you've ever seen me golf, you know what I mean. I don't have the golf balls any more. They're lost in a pond or deep in a forest somewhere.)

On the topic of golf balls, I heard of an advisor using a unique marketing twist. He joined an exclusive country club in order to meet people and tune up an otherwise awful golf game. Because of his poor play, he had dozens of golf balls custom-printed to read, "If found, please return to..." with his name and phone number. As the year unfolded, he lost countless golf balls, but not one person called him to say they had found one. However, whenever he introduced himself in the club house, he often would hear, "Hey, you're the guy with the golf balls!" So perhaps they can have impact and shelf life after all.

Other examples of advisors who have done a good job in this department:

An advisor told me of a good client who referred a family member to him. The advisor knew that the client had two teenage children, both of whom played classical instruments. To thank his client, the advisor sent two copies of the best-selling money management book, *The Wealthy Barber*, as well as four tickets to an upcoming symphony performance. The attached card read, "Thanks for waving my flag. I enjoy our relationship more than you know. Let's get the kids started with good financial planning strategies, and I hope all of you enjoy the show. It's the least I can do." The entire family was amazed. The children wrote the thank-you card to the advisor.

On another occasion, an advisor called to say that he had received a valuable referral from a client who was a successful business owner. In response to the question about what to send the client, I asked the advisor to tell me something about him. Apparently his international business was doing well, and he traveled extensively. Because of that, I suggested that the advisor send a one-year subscription of *Executive Summaries*. (Each month for a year, subscribers receive three to four of the best business books of the day, each summarized into four or six pages.) The advisor included a card that read, "Thank you very much for introducing Barbara to me. I know you travel and are very busy, but I also know you take pride in staying current. I thought this would be a small way to pass along my sincerest appreciation for your confidence in me." The client was amazed.

Another advisor called our office with news that he had received one of his biggest referrals ever from a terrific client. He asked what he should do to say thanks. On his client's FORM profile, which the advisor had faxed to us, we noted that the client had purchased a new motor home for West Coast trips with his wife. We suggested that the advisor send the client a one-year subscription to *RV World* magazine. Total cost to the advisor was $28. He sent it along with a thank-you card that read, "I just wanted to say thanks for introducing me to Bruce. We had a great meeting and he speaks very highly of you. I saw this magazine at a store the next day and couldn't resist. I remember you telling me about your motor home, so as a small token of my appreciation, I thought I'd send it along to say thanks."

Every month for the rest of the year, an issue of the magazine showed up at the client's door. Like any good hero story, this one has a happy ending. The same client has sent the advisor three additional referrals.

You can imagine the impact that good referral recognition has when combined with the new client welcome process. It can create a perpetual stream of referrals. As I mentioned earlier, most top advisors get all of their new clients by way of referrals. One such advisor told me that she informally tracks her clients' genealogies, meaning she charts her referrals. She has a client that is the ninth generation in a line tracing back to her preferred clients.

Milestone Recognition

Events that happen in your clients' lives are also worthy of your attention. Birthdays and anniversaries are a given. There are other special circumstances that you can recognize to show your clients that your relationship with them goes well beyond money.

One advisor spoke to a client who had just received a huge promotion. Not only was the client's income about to dramatically increase but so too were his pressures, stresses and responsibilities. The advisor send the client a congratulatory card and a copy of the book *The Fifth Discipline*, a great management and leadership book by Peter Senge. The client was beyond appreciative.

Another advisor learned that a client was having a huge family reunion. Being that the client was of Scottish descent, the advisor bought a simple coat of arms with a printed history of the family name and sent it to the client. It was present at the reunion and everyone attending heard of how it had come to be there.

One advisor sends his clients who become first-time parents and grandparents a framed stock certificate from Disney Corporation or Toys R Us. The card accompanying the gift reads: "Congratulations. Since you are probably going to keep this company in business during the years to come, you might as well own a piece of it. You can put it towards (child's name) education."

Another advisor once sent a copy of the book *The Richest Man in Babylon* to a good client's son who had just graduated from high school. The father called a few days later to say that he was amazed to see his son read the book in one sitting. It literally transformed the way the young man thought about money. The father joked that if *he* had given his son the book, it probably wouldn't have been read. But coming from the advisor directly with a congratulatory card got his attention.

If you see an article in the newspaper featuring a client's business, have it laminated and sent to the client. If a client achieves a meaningful investment milestone, frame a couple of pieces of foreign currency from the countries in which the client's money is invested and send it with a congratulatory card that says, "Congratulations on your milestone. Here is where some of your money works while you sleep at night."

The good client of an advisor we know mentioned that his family was excited about going to Disney World for the spring break. The advisor mailed to the client a copy of the book *How to Get the Most from Disney World* with a note wishing them all a great vacation. The family sent the advisor a post card from Disney World, thanking him.

To recognize a great client who was retiring, an advisor went back to his FORM profile where he discovered that the client was an avid reader who enjoyed historical fiction and biographies. Based on that information, the advisor contacted our office, where we took up the hunt in several rare book shops. We came up with a limited edition biography of William Lyon Mackenzie King that had been signed by the man himself. Not only was the gift an asset that would grow in value, but it also showed that the advisor was paying attention. What better gift to get from one's financial advisor! Certainly better than flowers or a box of chocolates.

The top client of one advisor announced that he was remarrying. The advisor bought a little book called *How to Live With Another*

Person. The client called, laughing that maybe he should have read it a lot sooner. Another advisor told me of a client who recently went through a family tragedy. I suggested he send the client a copy of the book *When Bad Things Happen to Good People* along with a note that read, "I know this is a tough time. If you need to talk, give me a call. I'm thinking about you." The client was deeply moved.

When you manage people's money, you wear several hats. Your clients care about how much you know, but they also want to know that you care. What has this got to do with financial planning? Nothing and everything. Relationships are the name of the game.

Client Delights

Not all advisors can see themselves recognizing client milestones. That's okay. I recommend, however, that all advisors rely on some variation of 'client delights.' Toyota created the phrase and discovered that unexpected but pleasant little surprises went a long way toward building customer loyalty. It was Chrysler that invented the cup holder for cars, but most manufacturers decided it was trivial or too dangerous to drink hot coffee while driving, so they opted not to use them. Toyota, however, decided that if people were going to drink coffee in their cars, they would give them a cup holder. Studies have proven that people would drive a Toyota for four years and when trade-in time came, they would shop around. If the car they were looking at didn't have a cup holder, it would adversely affect their decision. Imagine that, a decision to buy a $30,000 car influenced by a five-dollar piece of plastic.

You can't underestimate the impact of a little surprise. My wife and I went to a drive-through diner to order their famous hamburgers and milkshakes. When we pulled up, the attendant noticed our dog Splinter in the car with us. When she handed us our food, she included a dog biscuit. Anyone who knows my wife knows that if you want to win her over, just give her dog a treat. She'll be talking about that episode for years.

Other examples of client delights:

Fridge Magnets – As silly as it sounds, a fridge magnet can be a huge marketing tool. Never underestimate the power of the fridge. If you ever invite me to your house, within five minutes I'll be in your kitchen, looking at or in your fridge.

I'm not suggesting that you simply glue your business cards to several magnets. Have them customized and make them worthy of prime fridge space. The best format includes your logo top left, your name bottom left and your phone number bottom right. In the middle place a quote. People love quotes. My favourite, which also gets a tremendous response from clients, is by Sir Winston Churchill: "Saving is a very fine thing, especially if your parents have done it for you."

So select a quote that best suits your style and represents your message. Mark Twain, Thomas Edison and Gloria Vanderbilt have created memorable ones, which might be appropriate.

Give Them Something To Talk About

For two reasons, your December holiday letter is the best time to send a fridge magnet. First of all, people get more mail in December than at any other time. As they sift through their letters, the lumpy feel of the magnet gets their attention and compels them to open yours first.

Secondly, your clients will be networking and socializing with their inner circles of friends and family members more than at any other time of the year. Typically in the kitchen, FORM topics dominate their conversations. When the subject of money comes up in a conversation between your client and their best friends, you want your name to be automatically mentioned. Imprinting and little delights give them something to talk about.

Speaking of holidays, I suggest that you don't send a card in December (a letter yes, a card no). Send a Thanksgiving card instead. It's unexpected, and chances are you will be the only person who sends one. On the card, write, "I hope you, your family and your friends have a safe holiday weekend. I also want to say 'thanks' for a great relationship."

Another benefit of fridge magnets and Thanksgiving cards is that they fall under the 'economies of scale' category, meaning you can send them to all of your clients. If you want to be really specific, you can segregate certain blocks of clients by their family, occupational and recreational interests. For example, if you have thirty-two clients who like gardening, attach an article on gardening tips along with the letter you send. Include a hand written 'PS' or stick-on note that says, "I thought of you when I saw this."

Taking it a step further, use what are called "one-offs" for your top clients. This term means that you are sending something strictly for that client. For example, when an advisor was talking to one of his top clients, the client revealed that he had just bought a new Land Rover truck. The advisor logged it in the client's profile. A few weeks later, as the advisor was preparing to send out a letter to his clients, he was reminded of the truck when glancing through the profiles. He visited the local Land Rover dealership and bought a small Land Rover key chain. He tossed it into the envelope with a note that read, "Hope you're enjoying your new toy." The gift hadn't cost much but the impact was huge.

You'll learn about FORM-related client dinners in the next section. They too are a great way of showing your appreciation to top clients.

Let me qualify all of this. First, milestones and client delights will never replace personal contact. They are strategies to complement call rotations and things like client lunches. Secondly, fulfilling these details is a lot of work. You're going to be busy. So you have a few decisions to make. Do you only do this type of value-add for your top twenty-percent of clientele? Do you hire a marketing assistant who can help you keep track and implement everything?

As you will learn later when we examine ways to develop a marketing plan, I recommend that you contact your top clients at least once a month by way of phone calls, letters, newsletters and so on. Be certain that they are hearing from you more frequently and more dramatically than they are hearing from your competitors.

Chapter 2

The Power of Promotional Partnering

The Power of Promotional Partnering

When I lay out a marketing plan for a financial advisor, I first draw four to six columns on a sheet of paper. My objective is to help the advisor create multiple incomes streams, steady avenues of predictable income from four to six different sources. Each column is a pillar and represents a target market. In short, I'm trying to help the advisor diversify his or her business and build a strong foundation on solid pillars.

By now, you can probably guess what your most important pillar is: your clients. It is critical not to start building other pillars until this one is established. Competitor proofing, uncovering assets and stimulating referrals based on the Rule of 52 are vital activities.

Once you've built and fortified your client pillar, you can begin to extend your reach by focussing on your second pillar. Your second pillar consists of relationships with promotional partners, and here's why: nothing is more persuasive than a third-party endorsement. Just as clients are far better at persuading their acquaintances than you are, accountants, lawyers and other influential people can endorse you with amazing results as well. Wouldn't it be great to have a sales force of advocates waving your flag, without the associated hassles that come with being a sales manager?

The concept of promotional partnering is not new nor is it exclusive to the financial services business. Throughout the marketing world, companies are collaborating and establishing a variety of strategic alliances that benefit all involved. Everyone has their reasons for collaborating. The synergistic benefits include reduced marketing costs, stronger non-conflicting relationships and subtle and/or obvious endorsements of one another in the marketplace. Promotional partnering is probably the hatching ground for the phrase "working smart."

In big business, you see this trend more extensively than ever. I recently viewed a TV ad for Century 21, the real estate firm. The commercial began by saying that America Online, with sales in excess of one billion dollars, is the success story of the decade. The ad went on to say that Century 21, with real estate transactions in excess of one trillion, makes it the success story of the century. Obviously, Century 21 uses AOL, and to offset the costs of its ads or to receive favorable Internet services, the company subtly endorses AOL.

Speaking of television, not long ago I watched a hockey game via satellite between the New York Rangers, at home in Madison Square Gardens, and the visiting Dallas Stars. The game was televised on the Madison Square Gardens Network. (MSG, of course, owns the Rangers.) During a stoppage in play, a commercial came on, singing the praises of an American Express affinity card. This particular card featured a New York Rangers logo, promising card members special New York Rangers perks. I'm willing to bet that MSG gave AMEX a favourable air time rate in exchange for a commission that stemmed from fees and interest charges on the affinity cards.

Being a frequent flyer, I collect points on a number of airlines. Not long ago, *Maclean's* magazine offered me one thousand bonus points if I would subscribe to their magazine for a year. Air Canada is itself a major advertiser in *Maclean's*; you'll find the magazine offered regularly in its planes.

Everyone is getting into it. McDonald's occasionally offers a chocolate bar, pack of gum or a Beanie Baby toy when you buy one of their meal deals. The partnering companies love the exposure and hope that it leads to increased sales. Even *Seinfeld* got into the act with countless (and shameless) tie-ins with companies.

The Cornerstone to Success: Collaborating With Strategic Alliances

The most powerful aspect of promotional partnering is the endorsement that can be created. Like client referrals, when a banker, accountant, lawyer, leasing specialist or any other influential businessperson suggests that one of his or her clients call you, the toughest part of the sale has already been done. The likelihood of converting the person into becoming at least a customer is pretty good.

The first step for both emerging and established advisors is to create a network of promotional partners which, in time will bring value to the advisor. As a variation on the "pillar" metaphor, I use the analogy of a hub and spokes when it comes to partners. The advisor is the hub and each partner represents a spoke. As 'hub,' your job is to build a partnering wheel that will generate business for you. A little later in this section we'll look at the nuances of effective networking. For now, I'd like to talk about who your spokes should be.

I am absolutely convinced that your best partners might potentially be found among your existing clients. I therefore suggest you look inward. There is an old marketing maxim advising that you always pull in a direction where people are already pushing you. Chances are you have a few clients who think highly of you and would be more than receptive to take the relationship to the next level. At the risk of being overly repetitive, work with people who are already convinced.

In addition to generating new business, you further insulate your clients from competitive factors by partnering with them. When we examined the Loyalty Ladder, we learned that the more of a client's assets you manage, the more connected that person is to you. Partnering has the same effect. The bond you already have is fortified further with each layer you add to the relationship.

It's appropriate to recall at this point the Law of Reciprocity, which states that giving starts the receiving process. That said, if you want to stimulate more endorsements, you should get in the habit of endorsing.

I consider a couple of advisors I know to be power-brokers. They are always looking for ways to steer business to their business-owner clients. They always wrap up a meeting with a new client by asking for business cards and promising that they'll keep their ears and eyes open for opportunities to endorse them.

On occasion, we've taken the power-broker concept to the next level with some of our clients by rolling out what is called an REM campaign. REM stands for Reciprocal Endorsed Marketing, and it's really quite simple and effective.

Your Partner's Clients Are Great Prospects

Let's say an advisor has a great relationship with a client who owns a general insurance firm. The advisor makes reference, in either a letter or newsletter, that, "On a regular basis, a number of my clients ask if I know someone who offers home and auto insurance…." The endorsement subtly profiles the client who owns the general insurance firm. In return, the general insurance specialist will send out a similar letter to his clients, endorsing the financial advisor. This endorsement process can progress to future letters, combined luncheon or dinner seminars, you name it. After all, the other's clients are each other's best prospects.

Some advisors are wary of endorsing one specific firm. For example, an advisor might have four clients who sell general insurance. The advisor doesn't want to alienate three clients by endorsing just one.

For other advisors, their compliance department will not allow them to profile clients specifically. In these instances, we've circumvented the situation by rolling out a Client Network campaign.

In this campaign, the advisor sends out a brief questionnaire to all of his or her business-owner clients, requesting permission to endorse them when other clients inquire. All interested clients are asked to fill out a profile on their businesses and to return it to the advisor so that he or she can have a clear understanding of the types of services the clients' businesses provide. When the profiles are returned, the advisor creates a listing of the various services in a plasticized bookmark format. The bookmark does not give specific names, only services such as accounting, printing, landscaping, etc. This way, if the advisor has six accountants as clients, none will feel slighted. The bookmarks are sent to all clients along with a letter informing them that they should put the bookmark in their Yellow Pages. Should they ever need an expert, all they have to do is call their advisor, and he or she will see that they are well looked after.

This campaign attempts to position the advisor as the "crisis go-to" person in the clients' eyes. Let me use myself as an example. A client calls me. "Duncan, I received your letter and bookmark. Great idea. I know you've been harping on me to get my will updated. I have to take care of a few other things as well and, frankly, I'm a little disillusioned with my current lawyer. Whom do you recommend I call?" I proceed to put him on hold, dial up my legal client and conference in the three of us. After introducing the lawyer, I tell the client that several of my other clients work with her and are very pleased. I then ask the lawyer to take good care of the client, and I get off the line. Fifteen minutes later, the client invariably calls to thank me. A few days later, a card arrives from the lawyer, thanking me for the vote of confidence. For the rest of the week, she is thinking of how she can reciprocate. It's powerful. And what is doubly powerful is that I never once asked for a referral. In keeping with earning the right and imprinting, I have made an impact on the lives of two people, and they are both appreciative.

Similar stories abound. One advisor had a client ask if he knew anyone in the printing business. His daughter was getting married, and she needed an assortment of items printed. He put the client in touch with another client who owned a high-end printing business. The printer delivered a terrific job, and everyone walked away happy.

In another instance, an advisor was speaking with a client who had just been downsized. Financially, the client wasn't worried; he was just feeling a little dejected. The advisor put in a three-way call to another of his clients who was a career and business consultant. The consultant spent a bit of time with the unemployed client, helping him rebuild his confidence by assessing his skills and value in the marketplace. I don't need to tell you the pleasure everyone felt when the client was hired by a firm for a better position than the one he had held previously.

Expand Client Relationships Beyond Money

Interestingly, some advisors will not engage in this approach for fear that someone will make them look bad. It is a legitimate concern, but the likelihood of it happening is very low. A sailboat was meant to sail, not sit in the safety of the harbor. The benefits of this campaign are rewarding and far outweigh the risks.

The minimum that this concept can achieve is getting clients to think about making referrals and endorsements. Several advisors have told me that they have noticed an influx of referrals as a result of this campaign, even from people who never took advantage of it. A coincidence?

One of the best times to introduce this campaign is after a client survey. Once your clients have returned their surveys, send a thank-you letter for their participation. In the second paragraph, introduce the network idea, referring to the enclosed bookmark and suggest that clients put it in their Yellow Pages for future use. Even the clients who never take advantage of the offer will hold you in higher regard if for no other reason than you took the initiative. When it comes to client marketing, nothing goes unnoticed. Everything matters. Be proactive; your actions will pay dividends. But remember to stick with them; they will take time to gather steam.

An interesting variation on this approach is to help two clients collaborate with one another. It is very rewarding to introduce two clients and then watch them forge a meaningful business relationship or friendship. It is even more rewarding to see the results that stem from helping two clients launch an REM campaign. One advisor suggested that a chiropractor client should collaborate with an insurance specialist. The results were highly favourable for both.

Create A Client Advisory Council

As I mentioned earlier, another interesting way to partner with your clients is to create a Client Advisory Council or a board of directors. Invite about twelve clients (generally business owners and other favourites) to lunch or dinner and ask for feedback on how you can improve your services in order to attract clients as good as them. This roundtable approach can generate tremendous feedback and trickle-down business activity. Some advisors make it an even larger event; in addition to the brainstorming luncheon, the advisor states, "As successful business people, you are essentially here to represent my clients in helping me find ways to raise the bar…" Afterwards, in appreciation, a game of golf, boat cruise, sporting or arts event takes place, further bonding the group. They meet again six months later.

You might recall while I was outlining DART that I referred to client dinners as one more way to thank your clients in a meaningful and efficient manner. The bottom line is, good things happen when you talk to and get in front of your clients. Aside from call rotations, I have yet to find a more cost-effective way to competitor-proof clients, uncover assets and generate referrals. The key to these events being successful is in finding ways to make them compelling enough that your clients look forward to attending them. The biggest break-through I've seen with client dinners is to add a non-financial theme to them – in other words, making them fun!

Add Some Sizzle To Your Client Dinners

Not long ago, several advisors held client dinners that focused solely on financial information. They soon found that attendance was dwindling; clients weren't bringing guests as they once had. So they went back to the FORM profiles and looked for commonalties within the client group.

With one advisor, a significant number of his top clients indicated gardening as a hobby on their FORM questionnaires. The advisor also liked gardening and had a client who was a gardening and land-scaping expert with his own shop. The advisor sent a letter to the gardening clients with a headline at the top that read, "My clients are the pick of the crop." To ensure their attention, the advisor stapled a package of seeds to the page to create a lumpy-mail effect. The text of the letter stated that the advisor was holding a special client dinner to discuss ways of "growing your portfolio." The opening paragraph was laden with sowing, harvesting and other gardening metaphors. The next paragraph informed clients that after the advisor's fifteen-minute financial commentary, a guest speaker would provide tips on how to grow an outstanding garden. Draws would be held. The cost of admission playfully suggested that each client bring his or her spouse and a friend who liked gardening. The event was unbelievably successful.

Your FORM profiles can provide you with a raft of ideas. Find a cluster of clients with similar interests and link a non-financial theme (which obviously fits your style) with a financial one. Then get a client to be the guest presenter. The key is to offer something that you know your clients will like and make the event interesting.

Advisors have done "We Search the World for our Clients" events, in which the advisor talks about global investing and a client in the travel business talks about exotic travel destinations. Others have held events with a "Having a Portfolio that Sizzles" theme, in which the advisor holds the dinner in a private section of a nice restaurant and provides a brief but timely financial commentary. After dinner, the chef or restaurant owner, ideally a client, speaks to the guests about cooking and entertaining tips.

Another idea is to hold a "Financial Planning to a Tee" event at a golf and country club. The advisor gives a financial state-of-the-nation after which a golf pro tells memorable golfing stories and offers golf tips. The initial letter to clients can include a golf tee for a lumpy-mail effect. One advisor went so far as to include a small golf pencil with an eraser. The headline of the letter read, "You can erase a bad golf score, but it's harder to erase a financial mistake."

One advisor hosted a function whose theme was "Have a Smokin' Portfolio." The advisor spoke about shrewd investment decisions, and a client who imported cigars followed him with a presentation about the cigars of the world. Everyone received a sample, and a draw was held for a box of premium cigars. (I suggested that the advisor partner with a dry cleaner as well because of the resulting stench.)

Events such as "Fishing for Better Returns" can feature an expert from a fishing store. Those who attend can get a chance to use a fishing simulator. An event with the theme of "Building a Bridge to a Solid Financial Future" might feature a bridge-playing expert. Other theme events can include wine experts, bird-watching aficionados, professional photographers, decorating and home renovating consultants. The list is endless.

Educate And Entertain

Some advisors have told me that never in a million years would they hold this type of event. "I'm their financial advisor!" they tell me. "They want me to make them money and to keep them informed, not entertain them." I realize that this isn't for everyone. Do whatever moves you. But remember what Warren Buffett said: "The marketplace will pay you more to entertain it than it will to educate it." If your financial dinners are simply money-oriented, you might be disappointed unless, of course, you can get financial wizard George Soros to speak to your clients.

While your financial expertise is essential to your success, I'm convinced that some people don't want to know everything you know. We can compare this to electricity; I don't know how it works. I just turn on a switch and there it is. Some of your clients hire you to make all of their financial worries disappear, not necessarily wanting to know the details of how you do it.

That said, if you only want to highlight financial issues, be certain that you add sizzle in other ways. If you have a fund company wholesaler as a partner, suggest an exceptional event for twelve people rather than an average event for twenty-four. Exceed their expectations by meeting in a small up-scale restaurant and spoil your clients rotten. Have the wholesaler say a few words before it's your turn to speak.

But I'd like to ask you to at least consider using a client as a guest speaker at an event with a non-financial theme. Clients can make great promotional partners. These small affairs aren't intimidating, and they are manageable in terms of follow-up and generating great results. Remember, there is a direct correlation between how interesting your event is and how many clients will bring a guest.

Let's shift gears now and take a more panoramic view of promotional partnering. The same rules apply to partnering as they do to marketing; once you've done a good job with your existing clients, only then should you look further. You would never leave your clients twisting in the wind while you're looking for new clients. The same rationale should apply when you look for people with whom you can collaborate.

It goes without saying that an advisor should establish strategic alliances with at least one accountant and lawyer. Accountants are obvious gatekeepers to a lot of money. Few top-calibre investors will make any significant financial move without first discussing it with their accountants. Accountants are involved when a businessperson sells their company. They are called upon for advice when a client receives a severance package. Lawyers, in turn, handle inheritances and divorces. They are also involved in business transactions, severance packages and so on. Obviously, both professions bring a tremendous opportunity for collaboration in the area of estate planning. But where do you look to find good ones?

Your Clients Can Introduce You To Great Partners
Again, look within your client profiles. Several advisors have been surprised to find that six of their clients used the same accountant, and four others used the same lawyer. You can approach those potential partners from a position of strength because a peripheral connection already exists.

If you are not fortunate enough to have clients clustered with the same accountants and lawyers, call your best clients and ask them if they would recommend their professionals, perhaps even make the introduction.

Some advisors hold their annual client reviews at the offices of their clients' accountants. In addition to giving the accountants a sense of involvement, it lets the advisor scrutinize potential partners.

You have to be mindful not to arouse any skepticism in broaching the concept of collaborating. Be aware that these are analytical people driven more by a fear of loss than the possibility of a gain. When you initiate a conversation and make your intentions clear, unspoken objections begin swirling around in their minds. It is essential that you market yourself rather than sell yourself. There is a critical distinction.

Therefore, it is important that you approach a partner via a referral rather than out of the blue. Also, as with all forms of marketing, never bring your needs to a potential partner. Bring your skills and your unique value.

When you first make contact, introduce yourself and explain that you work with a number of people who regularly require the services of the prospective partner's profession. Offer to take that person to lunch so that you can discuss a potential reciprocal alliance. Explain your area of expertise. Ask if he or she has an existing relationship with an advisor and if so, how it is working out. Try to discover the person's hot buttons.

Uncover Their Hot Buttons

What are 'hot buttons' in this case? Let me explain. While rare, some lawyers and accountants frankly don't need any more business; they have all they can handle. (This is changing. Like most businesses, it is becoming increasingly competitive for accountants and lawyers. More of them are beginning to open up to new opportunities.) However, some accountants and lawyers just want to find someone whom they can trust to make them look good in the eyes of clients they refer. That is their 'hot button.' For others, their hot button might be in finding creative ways to bring intangible value to their clients. Whatever the case may be, search for these triggers and home in on them.

Several advisors that we've worked with have become frustrated because they could not get a prospective partner to warm up to their offer, even if that person should have. In one such instance the advisor, who wanted to position himself as an estate-planning authority, approached an accountant and a lawyer, both of whom were already doing business with some of the advisor's clients. Neither seemed enthused by the offer to work closely with the advisor. We told him not to worry, that this was a typical example of an accountant and lawyer who just don't 'get it.' They couldn't see the big picture. After explaining to him that it was important he not look needy in the eyes of these prospective partners, we suggested that he do something dramatic to get their attention as well as to demonstrate his code of conduct.

The advisor called each prospective partner's secretary to begin the "ally-building" process. (It's important to get to know the frontline staff in order to create a friendly bond. They can often become terrific inside champions, helping you rally the prospective partner.) The advisor told both secretaries that he wanted to buy some of their bosses' time, that he had clients who often needed to a have a second opinion on a variety of issues including off-shore structuring, real estate transactions, corporate tax concepts, drawing up a will and so on. The advisor explained that he wanted to have some of their time "in inventory" so that if clients of his needed a lawyer or accountant, as their advisor he could provide those services and therefore look like a hero.

Later that day, both the accountant and lawyer called the advisor back. The advisor told each of them, "I know a number of people who can use your services. I can look good by giving them an hour of your time 'on me.' I'm sure that once you get in front of them, they will do business with you. If you feel that you are getting good value and that sometime down the road you feel inclined to reciprocate by endorsing my services to your clients, I'll make you look good. You can hold me accountable. If you choose not to send anyone to me, that's okay too. At least we had a chance to give it a try."

Today all three have a good relationship and often actually collaborate with a life insurance specialist on estate planning symposiums. Just so you know, the advisor used a process called "risk reversal" or "the puppy dog close." Each prospective partner had nothing to lose and everything to gain by giving the advisor a try. It got the attention of each and, as I mentioned earlier, made a serious statement about the advisor's code of conduct.

Treat Partners As You Would Your Best Clients

I'm not suggesting that all relationships will unfold that quickly and smoothly. Other prospective partners may take longer to "see" the value and get over any imagined downside they feel might ensue from the alliance. My suggestion is to treat a prospective partner as you would a prospective client. Start a FORM profile and nurture the relationship.

What's really exciting about partnering is that it's not only accountants and lawyers who have influence over people in the marketplace. I encourage all advisors to build a network consisting of a wide cross-section of business people. Every advisor needs one.

The term 'network' conjures up a variety of images for different people. You'll be glad to know that I'm not advising that you don a fez and roam around a Shriners' luncheon, pumping hands and swapping business cards. Networking is a process of continually cultivating and nurturing relationships for the purposes of a *quid pro quo* benefit. A typical network consists of a group of people from various walks of life who believe in each other and are, for lack of a better word, "influencers." This simply means that when they meet someone in need of the services you offer, they will endorse you without hesitation. A network also consists of people who would walk to the ends of the earth for you should you ever find yourself against a wall.

As mentioned, a good network consists of like-minded people who share a common goal – to further develop themselves and their businesses. In the listing of a typical network that follows, all of these professions have individuals who can bring great value to an advisor:

- Accountant
- Lawyer
- Real Estate Agent
- General Insurance Broker
- Business Consultant
- Chiropractor
- Architect
- Leasing Specialist
- Mortgage Broker or Banker
- Travel Specialist
- High-Calibre Concierge
- Media, Advertising and PR Specialist
- City Councilor

There are a plethora of other niche specialists besides these. For example, an advisor who works with chiropractors can partner with an accountant who specializes in working with health professionals — a perfect match.

Since you're the engine driving your network, I highly recommend that you build FORM profiles for each of your partners as it grows and evolves. As with clients, you will want to bring value to them, and in order to bring value that will have any impact, you have to discover what it is that they value.

Mastermind

As your network gathers momentum, I encourage that you hold regular mastermind luncheons or breakfasts on a quarterly or monthly basis. These sessions will enable you to "rally the troops" and keep your finger on the network's pulse. In his timeless book, *Think and Grow Rich*, Napoleon Hill passes along ideas for what he calls the "Mastermind Alliance." Jim Rohn refers to the concept as the Law of Expanded Association. Surrounding yourself with good people will serve you well as you continue to develop yourself and your business.

Most advisors do not have more than one person per sector in their network. The depth of one relationship is more important than how many you have. And there is no limit to the size of an advisor's network. As with most things, eighty percent of your network referrals will stem from twenty percent of the people in your network.

Speaking of which, the criteria for joining your network is not limited solely by a person's ability to send you business. Different people can bring different forms of value to you. Some will provide a good sounding board, helping you from becoming mired in minutiae. Others can make you look good when a client calls for help. (Like the time a panicky client called his advisor, looking for a good veterinarian for his very sick dog. The advisor linked him up with a client who is a top vet. The dog is fine, by the way.)

I mentioned networking luncheons earlier. I don't want it to sound as if they aren't a good use of time. I know several advisors who are members of organizations like the Kiwanians as well as others such as the Chamber of Commerce, Young Entrepreneurs and so on. A number of people have told me that they have networked and collaborated with excellent people that they first met at these functions. If face-to-face networking interests you, read on. If not, fast-forward a couple of pages.

Here are a couple of essential networking strategies:

Have a compelling sound bite. As an entrepreneur, you will meet new people in a variety of settings. Invariably, you will meet people who ask what you do. Don't simply say that you are a financial advisor. Wake them up with a compelling statement.

For example, I know one advisor who can be in a crowd of people he's never met and within minutes, create a small circle of people leaning in to hear his story. Initially, he makes no reference to the fact that he's a financial advisor. He often cryptically explains that he "makes millionaires." He then proceeds to talk intelligently about events around the world and how they shape his decisions. His introductory sound bite is intriguing, and his comments are compelling because they paint pictures that have some drama and sizzle. I'm not suggesting that you have to be the world's most engaging conversationalist, but as concerns all presentations, whether they be to one person or one hundred, don't wing it. You must be somewhat rehearsed and have your thoughts clearly organized.

Have a great memory. My weakness has been my memory for names. It is so impressive when you can remember the name of someone you once met briefly. According to Dale Carnegie, the sweetest sound to a person's ears is his or her own name being said. But my memory is funny. I'm sure you can relate when I say that I can remember some things incredibly well while others never seem to sink in. I've studied memory-building techniques rather extensively and frankly, much of what I've learned is hard to implement on a daily basis.

To help me, I've created my own (big surprise) acronym – AREA – that serves me reasonably well. When I first meet someone, I try to use one or more of four techniques to memorize that person's name and important aspects of the conversation.

The A stands for Associate. When someone tells me his or her name,

I immediately associate it with something. For example, I was working at home on my laptop when a woman telephoned, wishing to speak with my wife who was out at the time. The caller's name was Katrina, and she wanted to set up a business meeting with my wife. I immediately thought of the 1980s music group, Katrina and the Waves, who sang the song, "I'm Walking on Sunshine." Instantly, that song came to mind where it stayed, stuck, until my wife came home. (Of course, I could have written her name down, but that would have messed up my acronym.) Songs and scenes are especially memorable because our internal dialogues tend to be in pictures and rhythms. At least mine are.

The R stands for Repeat. If I don't have an instant association with which to work, I'll sometimes repeat the person's name in my mind. While not a bad technique, it lacks personality.

The E stands for Exaggerate. I'll give you an example. My wife and I were out for a walk when we met a couple driving past in their Jeep. When they saw our dog, they slowed down. We waved, they stopped and we all introduced ourselves. After they had pulled away, my wife and I continued our walk. A few seconds later, she rattled off a silly verse: "Joanne and Guy driving in their Jeep. And Joanne is sitting in the passenger seat." It sounds corny, but it worked.

Speaking of corn, the second A in AREA stands for animate, as in cartoons. For example, I headed out to the store one day to pick up a few items for home. Among other things on my mental list were some ant killer for the garden and a picture frame hanger. In a hurry to beat closing time and without a pen and paper, I visualized a giant ant hanging a picture in our foyer. As bizarre as it sounds, it really works (plus the ant did a great job). Combine the exaggeration and animation elements together to create a vivid, panoramic image of what you are trying to recall. Incidentally, the great Roman orators used this visualization technique to recall six-hour speeches. It was so helpful, they could actually deliver an entire speech backwards. (That *would* be helpful.)

Contact Management

The key to nurturing good relationships is to diligently use a good contact management system. Create FORM profiles for everyone in your network and use FORM to guide you in making unique contacts with them. Create a variation of a call rotation just to stay in touch with your contacts. As with clients, the frequency should be higher and the impact of the contact more dramatic based on the level of the relationship you have. Don't take the call-rotation concept too literally. It's really a communication rotation you're aiming for, meaning you'll use the phone, mail, e-mail, to send a variety of relevant information. The key is to be consistent and unique.

To be unique, you need to be thoughtful. For example, if a person in your network is of Norwegian descent, send them a newspaper clipping regarding the Narvik Sun Pageant that takes place each

February. Ivy day in Ireland is October 6; Mahatma Gandhi was born on October 2. (You might know people who would appreciate you acknowledging those dates.) If you network with someone in the medical profession, send that person a card on World Health Day in April. There are no limits if you are imaginative. Buy an almanac for ideas and let them rip.

Turn Vendors Into Partners

An interesting trickle-down benefit of networking is that you can learn how to turn a vendor into a partner. As you get further into the partnering mindset, you will find yourself thinking, "Who can I involve in this marketing initiative that will bring me value as well as benefit to themselves by becoming involved with me?" For some advisors, partnering becomes a healthy obsession. The following examples will explain what I mean.

A financial advisor called for advice regarding a marketing initiative. He was targeting high-calibre dentists and had decided to set up a booth at an annual dental trade show. Seeing as his clients and prospects would likely attend, I agreed that it would be a good idea. My concern, however, was that I didn't want him simply to show up and stand around a fishbowl for two days. I wanted him to own the show and for his booth to stand out in the crowd. I asked the advisor, "What do dentists love to do?" He immediately answered, "Golf." I said, "Exactly" and told him to set up a golf net beside his booth that dentists could use to drive golf balls. He agreed that it was a good idea but was uncertain about where to get the net. I called the regional manager for a well-respected golf store and asked if he would do it. My logic was that thousands of dentists would also be great prospects for the store.

The golf store manager saw the big picture and jumped at the opportunity. At the show a month later, I rode the escalator to the mezzanine of the convention centre where all the booths were set up. As I neared the top, I could hear a steady "whack!" the melodious sound of golf balls being drilled into a net. Nearing the advisor's booth, I observed a respectable crowd standing around the net. People were laughing, and one dentist told the advisor that this was the first time he had ever had fun in all the times he'd ever been to the show.

My point is, how much did it cost the advisor for the net? Nothing; the golf store picked up the tab. Even better, they also provided a couple of professional golfers to give tips as well as a couple of great prizes for draws. It was a hugely successful event.

Fly fishing or golf simulators can also work well for several advisors who have hosted booths at medical trade shows. See what's out there and use it.

Partners And Sponsors
Holding seminars on the topic of marketing strategies for business-owner clients is a sure-fire way to solicit sponsorship by lawyers,

accountants, printing companies and so on. I've been the guest speaker at a breakfast seminar for an advisor's best entrepreneurial clients and prospects. The local Chamber of Commerce was so enthused that it endorsed the event as a Chamber function, promoting it as well as arranging the facility and catering services. The end result was a virtually hands-free event for the advisor attended by more than two hundred people.

In one instance, a female advisor hosted a series of six lunch-and-learn seminars featuring a variety of speakers, including a self-defense expert, time management specialist, a communications consultant and others. All of the speakers were members of a Women's Business Network and spoke *pro bono* in exchange for the opportunity to network. The Women's Business Network sponsored the event, charging a small fee to help offset costs and promoting the event in their newsletter. It was great partnering all around.

Other Pieces To The Partnering Puzzle

Another advisor promoted a unique event to his clients, many of whom were either retired or on the verge of retiring. Rather than bring in a financial speaker, he offered a retirement lifestyle seminar that focused on the non-financial aspects of retirement. Because relationships, self-esteem, one's meaning and purpose in life, as well as other psychological elements, are affected in retirement, he felt this unique approach would be well-received. He selected a humorous yet well-qualified speaker and approached typical sponsors such as an accounting office and law firm. However, since the advisor wanted to use the event for prospecting as well, he needed ways to attract interesting people to the event. He executed a well-targeted geographic direct mail campaign and approached the local newspaper to see if it was interested in becoming involved. Because of the event's uniqueness and the fact that it was certain to attract a high-quality audience, the newspaper opted to provide several thousands of dollars worth of free advertising in exchange for exposure at the event and tickets to offer to key advertising clients.

Other advisors have done similar events but added a radio station to sponsor and provide ads as well. In another situation, an advisor made the cost of admission a jigsaw puzzle or toy that could be donated to the local Toys for Tots campaign. The theme for each of these seminars was, "There are several pieces to the retirement puzzle. Are you getting the complete picture?" (Hence the jigsaw puzzle donation request.) On the last page of his next newsletter the advisor ran a picture of dozens of toys piled up outside the door of the room to pay tribute to those involved.

So start thinking about ways you can initiate promotional partnering. You will enjoy the proceeds and, most importantly, you will enjoy the process. There are few things more gratifying in business than expanding your horizons and bringing value to someone else along the way.

Looking Out for Number One

As an entrepreneur, I'll be the first to tell you that you should always take care of the only thing you can control, yourself. Here's why: I have worked with advisors who have had to use the "tools of last resort," meaning that they have had to confront or disassociate from certain partners who took more than they were giving back. One advisor sponsored an accounting firm's golf tournament to the tune of several hundred dollars. The advisor was livid when he discovered that all he would get in exchange was the sponsorship of one hole, a green fee to play golf and dinner. He confronted his partner, someone the advisor had sent a lot of business to but frankly hadn't received much from in return. After a rather heated exchange the accountant relented, allowing the advisor to organize a golf clinic by the resident golf pro. Forty-five minutes before the shotgun start, those interested received golf lessons, competed in a skills competition and had their names entered into a draw. During dinner, the advisor was thanked by one of the heads of the firm for his contribution, and during the few weeks that followed he generated more business via the accounting firm than during the six months prior.

So you live by the rules you set. If you play fair with someone who plays fair in return, you can enjoy the magic of the Law of Reciprocity. It truly is a powerful phenomenon, but you have to make it a habit and keep the faith as it gathers momentum. Take a clue from Lou Holtz, former coach of Notre Dame. He always ends a conversation by saying, "Is there anything I can do for you?" Your partners and those in your network have clients, and those clients are some of your best prospects. You will be endorsed if you have earned the right.

Putting It All Together With Newsletters

A newsletter is one of the most efficient tools you can use to tie all of your promotional partnering initiatives together vis à vis your client and prospect marketing efforts. The reason why I say "efficient" is because you can take advantage of the economies of scale and achieve a timely and topical message with the benefits of reasonable shelf life.

I have convinced a number of advisors not to have a brochure printed but rather to invest that money in a newsletter. My rationale is that a brochure is generally a 'feature dump' that is static and boring in singing the praises of the advisor. You have to remember that people today are well-informed and skeptical. Most brochures are written primarily for the benefit of the advisor; in no way do they contribute to the marketing bottom line.

All marketing must pay for itself and ultimately deliver many benefits. A quarterly newsletter does that. You can keep your clients "close to the fire" and validate for them that they are with the right person. It is a useful tool for bridging and fortifying partnerships. You can create a nagging feeling in the minds of prospects that they might be with the wrong person and should consider making a move.

But before I tell you what I think a newsletter should look like, let me tell you what it should not look like. I highly recommend that you do not use a 'boiler plate' or "off the rack" type newsletter, meaning a mass-produced, off-the-shelf piece with your picture screened in at the top but whose language is generic and contains bland 'investmentese.' Combine that with the fact that most of these generic newsletters have what are called 'stock model' pictures. One I saw recently had a picture of a 'typical family,' Dad with his sweater draped over his shoulder, Mom with a big smile on her face and the kids chasing a loping golden retriever through a park. It looked like the cover of a Sears catalogue.

While the version I just described is inexpensive and better than nothing, you can do so much more. Remember, you should be promoting the messenger, not just the message. But what do most newsletters promote? The message! And it's usually a pretty boring message at that. (Your clients don't say, "Heh, honey, look. Another article on dollar-cost averaging. This is great!") I am convinced that if you send out a run-of-the-mill version, your clients might appreciate receiving it, but they probably won't read it. Human nature says that facts tell but *stories* sell.

I strongly encourage you to hire a professional who will create a fully-customized newsletter. It will cost you more money, but cost should really only be a concern if there is a poor return on your investment. It's not the cost of a newsletter that's the issue; it's what it's worth. If cost really is of concern, you would still be better off with a one-page (printed front and back) customized newsletter than with a folded two-page generic piece.

Newsletters Affect All Facets Of Your Marketing Approach

If I were an advisor, the last thing I would want is for one of my clients to receive a newsletter from a competitor that looks just like mine. Even more than that, I would only want to send out a piece that I was proud of, one that I knew my clients would receive in the mail, open eagerly and devour.

As for prospects, I'd want my newsletter to be far more impressive than the one they are getting from their current advisor. I'd want to give them a tangible item that they could use to contrast me with their current advisor. People only switch advisors if they are dissatisfied with their current situation. A newsletter can help in that respect.

For my partners, I'd want to give them something more interesting than business cards or bland brochures to hand to their clients so that they would be inspired to take action.

That said, I suggest that half of your newsletter contain investment-related information and the other half contain human interest and community information. For human interest, include pictures and information about people and events that are of interest on a day-today level. For community feel, show that you are grateful for the community in which you live and that you want to give something back.

As Always, Start With Your Clients

Rent a wave pool for your clients' kids, grandkids, nieces, nephews and even their neighbors' kids. Make the cost of admission a can of food for the Food Bank. Take a picture of the children around the Food Bank truck with a big box of food about to be loaded into it.

Profile a client. If you have a great relationship with a client who is in business for him or herself, profile that client's firm in your newsletter. (Be sure that compliance regulations allow it.)

If you sponsor the soccer team of a client's child, put the team picture in the back of your newsletter. If someone on your office team marries, put a picture of the happy couple on the back page with a headline that reads, "New Merger Announced." Profile the achievements of your clients and their kids.

There are all kinds of value-adds you can include in your newsletter to give it extra sizzle and personality. Pictures of events, an upcoming event calendar, kids' stock pick contest updates, trivia questions, cartoons, your team picture and quotes are some suggestions. If A&E is profiling Warren Buffett during the upcoming season of *Biography*, note it in your newsletter. If you have new additions to your Lending Library, list the titles. I know of an advisor who had a great recipe for guacamole. The advisor printed it, complete with instructions to speed up the ripening process of avocados by putting them in a paper bag for a day or two at room temperature. Clients loved it.

Don't forget that your partners can play a role in your newsletter as well. If you have a promotional partnership with an accountant, and she can effectively articulate a timely tax issue, have her write an article accompanied by her picture. Your partner will be that much more inclined to endorse you to her clients by using your newsletter. It can also complement a Reciprocal Endorsed Marketing campaign.

Three-hole punch your newsletter so that clients can save it in their Welcome Kit binders. Ask your clients regularly if they know a friend or family member who would enjoy receiving a copy. If the newsletter is interesting, the likelihood they'll show their friends rises dramatically.

Audio Newsletters – Be Seen And Heard

If you really want to be adventurous, consider an annual audio newsletter as well. A car is a captive environment and for the most part, people still enjoy learning while they drive. Unlike the audio cassette business card that is essentially a glorified infomercial, an audio newsletter is far more informative, far more impressive and a lot less expensive. It doesn't require fancy packaging to get someone's attention because it is sent only to predisposed targets.

It is best to produce and distribute them in January. The content and format are really quite simple. A popular theme is, "Where do we go from here?" or "Sound Advice." On the A side of the cassette, the advisor gives his or her financial state-of-the-nation. The text can begin with the advisor discussing ways to invest events of the past year into those of the upcoming year. An interview with a fund manager, a well-known author or a similar type of authority can follow. These professionals are surprisingly accessible. An interview with a partner who discusses tax strategies or estate planning is also an idea. The B side is usually reserved for an edited recording of a seminar presented or orchestrated by the advisor. If that is not available, a Q&A would suffice.

Don't be intimidated by the recording and production process. Many advisors erroneously conclude that it's too complex a project to even consider. With today's technology, a good studio can make you sound superb – professional, astute, in command of your facts. Using digital technology, technicians can edit your stumbles and mistakes. Your interviews can be done on the telephone or they can be recorded separately and mixed later. For a surprisingly low fee, you can have as many copies as you need duplicated while retaining the master for future reproductions.

When you send a copy to a client, include a second cassette or a card that reads, "Several of my clients have friends who would benefit from this information. If you know someone who would enjoy his or her own copy, go ahead and give that person (enclosed card or cassette). If he or she is a friend or family member, the cassette is on me."

You've just made it easy for your client to endorse you to a close friend or two. When you bring on a new client, the cassette is a nice complement to your Welcome Kit. A second copy can be provided to make it easy for your new client to wave your flag.

It works the same way with promotional and network partners. The cassette has a lot more sizzle than a business card, and they will feel good about handing them out, especially if they themselves are featured on it.

For prospecting, the cassette becomes a tangible call-to-action. As you will learn in the next section on prospecting, a cassette can be a great tool in converting a prospect to a customer.

As an intellectual property, the audio newsletter has considerable shelf life, is unique and makes it easy for people to introduce you. It takes something abstract and makes it tangible. After dinner at a restaurant, I usually decline the offer of dessert when the server asks. On the few occasions that the server approaches me with a tray, asking, "Which one would you like?" I often choose one. Why? Because the server made it easy for me to select. He took the abstract of the word 'dessert' and made it tangible.

Your newsletters are important vehicles of communication that serve to fortify relationships and open new doors. If you are interested in the concept but concerned about who will actually do the work, later in the book I'll look at the importance of outsourcing and hiring an assistant. I'll also mention that some ideas, like these, are hard to measure. In this case, it usually comes in the form of positive feedback from your clients, partners and prospects. My experience tells me that good feedback is usually the activity preceding productivity.

Chapter 3

The Lost Art of Prospecting

The Lost Art Of Prospecting

I've come to realize that there are two important laws that must be respected when it comes to prospecting. The first is the Law of Attraction. A mentor of mine once said, "We are all magnets, and anything we want to have in our lives we must attract. We can't chase what we want because often what we chase eludes us. You certainly don't chase prospective clients because the more often you push them, the more you repel them." He added that if I wanted to attract more attractive clients, I would have to work at making myself more attractive to them than their current provider.

The Law of Attraction is the centerpiece of this section and the heartbeat of the entire book. My objective is to provide you with a variety of proven techniques that you can translate into results. There are many ideas out there, all of which will garner you degrees of success. You need to be unreasonably selective in choosing only the activities that will attract the clients you want and improve your results overall.

Even flawed activities can create a certain measure of productivity. You could tell your marketing assistant to call someone you've never spoken with before, to tell them you're returning that person's call. It will get you a result (albeit a weird one). Or when you leave a parking lot, if the car behind you looks expensive, pay the parking attendant for both your parking as well as the car behind you. Give the attendant a little extra on the condition that he or she passes the driver your card as you pull away. On the card write, "You should see how I treat my clients." That will get you a result as well. If you see an expensive car parked at a meter that has expired, drop a few coins in the meter. Leave your card on the windshield with the message that you hate parking tickets as well and took the liberty when you saw the meter had expired. Again, you'll get a result.

Don't get me wrong; I'm not endorsing these ideas. But what's my point in outlining these silly marketing tactics? It's to impress upon you that no matter what you do, you will get a result. The key, however, should be in selecting ideas that make the most sense to your situation and make you attractive to the marketplace.

The Professional Path Of Least Resistance

What I would like to propose is that you "stir the pot," so to speak, in as professional, efficient and fulfilling a manner as possible. I can't help but think of Viktor Frankl, author of the classic book *Man's Search for Meaning*. In his studies, Frankl developed a Task Implementation Model shaped as a box. He suggested that all human activities be categorized as belonging in one of four quadrants within the box.

Envision a box divided into four sections. The top left quadrant would consist of activities that are hard to learn and hard to do.

Open-heart surgery or building a satellite transmitter would fall within this category. The quadrant on the top right holds activities that are hard to learn but actually easy to do. For some people, driving a car with a manual transmission would apply. The quadrant on the bottom left contains activities that are easy to learn but actually hard to do. Physical labor and, for me, golf would fit that description. The quadrant on the bottom right consists of the activities that are easy to learn and easy to do. This is the quadrant that appeals to me. You'll be glad to discover that all the activities we'll be discussing belong in this corner.

Effective prospecting is more about finesse than force. Based on the Loyalty Ladder we discussed earlier, your objective is to select and sift good prospects from a mass of suspects. Once you've identified who your prospects are, you want to convert them into becoming customers. But here is my real point: you can't want them to become a customer more than they do. As I said earlier, it's like mining for gold; you have to move a lot of dirt to find an ounce of gold. You can't turn dirt into gold. I see advisors beat their heads against walls, trying to convince prospects to come onside. They grudgingly plow through a list of names, hoping to stumble upon someone who will give them an ear. It reminds me of salmon swimming upstream. It's inspiring to see them frantically going against the current, smacking against the rocks, avoiding the various dangers ahead of them. But for what? When they have finished their noble deeds, they die! Since you are not a salmon, you can choose to swim with the current. And here's how:

Get Focused

As a marketer, you have unique assets. In marketing jargon, these assets are referred to as your Unique Selling Proposition (USP). A USP can be defined as the momentum you have already established in your business. Or it can be aspects of your experience and your contacts, for example. Some advisors have an obvious USP. A person who ends a successful career as an aerospace engineer in order to become a financial advisor has a unique asset – an ability to connect with and persuade other engineers to become clients. An advisor of Dutch descent has a USP in terms of his ability to connect with the Dutch community in his city. These are obvious examples. For other advisors, closer examination is required to reveal their USP.

A universal aspect of a USP is that it relates to the messenger, not the message. In very few instances is a product, service or financial expertise unique to an advisor. For all intents and purposes, the message is widely available. For every advisor with whom we've worked, their USP has had something to do with themselves – the messengers.

Build On Your Strengths And Existing Momentum

So to reinforce the point I just made, an advisor's USP usually stems from the momentum he or she already has going. To quote Warren Buffett: "To swim a fast hundred meters, it's better to swim with the tide than it is to work on your stroke." Look to where you already have momentum. If you are like most advisors, a good starting point could be right under your nose.

As I have mentioned on several occasions, your clients might in fact be your best prospects. They might have needs being fulfilled elsewhere because it hasn't occurred to them to use you. Maybe they don't even know you offer certain products and services. Whatever the case may be, before you start trying to convince new prospects, work with the people who are already convinced and move them further up the ladder.

Your clients are the "tide," to play off Warren Buffett's quote. The fact that they are already onside ensures that they will be receptive. New prospects are more skeptical. I said it earlier: pull in the direction that people are already pushing you. It baffles me why some advisors don't buy into this philosophy. I see it all the time, advisors who bring on a customer or client, and that's as far as they take it. The advisor gets back on the prospecting and client-acquisition treadmill.

So look to your clients. The more you have to offer, the less likely it is they will ever leave.

Toyota realized this several years ago. Toyota owners were among the most satisfied of all car owners. People fresh out of college would start with a Corolla, then buy a Camry once their families came along. The only problem was, when the kids grew up and got their own cars or moved out, when the Toyota owners found themselves earning more money, sitting on a nice nest egg with more disposable income, they started longing for more than a Toyota. Toyota's answer? Extend their line. They created Lexus to compete with Mercedes, BMW and Jaguar. It's not surprising that a lot of Lexus owners are former Toyota owners.

Is Fee-Based An Issue For You?

But line extensions go beyond selling additional services. You may find yourself in a situation where you want to change the way you are compensated. More and more, advisors are either considering or implementing fee-based remuneration. If you change to a managed-money approach, you have to decide how you will approach your clients. Will you abruptly change or will you do so transitionally? Do you remember when Nissan once was Datsun? That slow and methodical transition took a long time to transpire. The objective was to ensure that the marketplace didn't notice or get spooked by the change. Whatever your approach, the most important consideration is that your clients not perceive *you* as the *real* benefactor in the change by the way in which you serve them.

Most advisors we've worked with approach their clients individually to introduce the fee-based concept. They start by explaining how they currently are paid, how each transaction involves a commission. They mention how some advisors use this system to their advantage by adopting a 'SWAT' marketing philosophy (SWAT= Sell What's Available Today). In other words, whatever stock the company has the most of ends up being "the greatest stock in the world." They then explain that, until recently, the fee-based approach was only available to elite investors. Today, because of demographic shifts, it is now open to "middle class" or aspiring investors. The benefits to clients are that they now essentially get their own fund managers who are even more accountable. The advisor does not have a vested interest in individual transactions. The advisor focuses more on an investment philosophy. Transactions become a means to end, not the end itself. Fees are clearly defined and specific. The advisor then contrasts the transaction approach versus the fee approach, illustrating with examples that benefit the client.

In heading off the cost objection, the advisor points out that costs appear high, but in reality it isn't what something costs but rather what it's worth. For example, when Picasso was asked to sketch the portrait of a wealthy young lady in Paris, he accepted the proposal and proceeded to sketch her portrait. It took all of five minutes. Shocked, the client challenged Picasso's fee of five thousand francs. She objected to paying so much for something that only took five minutes to complete. Picasso responded by saying, "It took me all my life to paint that."

Shifting Gears

Once you have done a good job prospecting to your clients, think of your pure prospecting pillars.

Before an advisor embarks on a prospecting campaign, I ask that he or she clarify whom it is they are trying to attract. I encourage the advisor to create an Ideal Client Profile.

On a sheet of paper, list the qualities you desire in a new client. What should the client's investment philosophy be? What personality style should he or she have? How many assets? (I can remember one advisor telling me that he only looks for clients with portfolios consisting of several commas.)

If you need help compiling this profile, think for a moment about your best clients. What is it about them you like so much? Is it because they empower you to implement your investment philosophy? Is it because they can easily justify your fee-based approach? Perhaps it's because they aren't always following the herd and chasing yesterday's winner.

Chances are your favorite clients are either business owners or recently retired. I always suggest that advisors make entrepreneurs a primary prospecting pillar. Why? If you read Tom Stanley's book *The Millionaire Next Door*, you already know that business owners are, for the most part, the highest quality and lowest maintenance clients out there. They are loyal. They have an 'invest' rather than 'consume' mentality, they are frugal without being cheap and they are prudent. But it isn't just what you get by targeting entrepreneurs; it also what you become. They can teach you a lot about life and business. They've seen it all. They've endured the peaks and valleys that come with being an entrepreneur. Nothing scares them.

Better than that, they also refer people just like themselves. Remember, the Law of Environment says that people generally hang out with, work with, live near and ultimately refer people like themselves.

An important component of your Ideal Client Profile is a section dedicated to what are called Knock-Out Factors. These are the characteristics and personality traits that you want no part of, such as 'stock jockeys,' 'do-it-yourselfers,' clients who insist on using more than one advisor and so on. Assuming that you plan to be in the business for a while and also assuming that you work hard, you have earned the right to be selective. (Your Ideal Client Profile and Knock-out Factors should apply to your existing clients as well.)

Some financial advisors have too many clients. Or, as I stated earlier, they have clients who are costing them more than they are bringing them. As such, the advisor might have to make some room. It's common for me to meet an advisor who for years has taken on anyone. The time comes, however, where that approach starts to hurt more than help. There comes a time in every top-producing advisor's life when he or she has to examine whether or not the current path is a slippery slope.

Avoid The Slippery Slope
Measurable progress stems from being more efficient and productive

over a reasonable period of time. Your output should start to decrease as your returns begin to increase. But being solely fixated on new client acquisition can lead to spontaneous combustion. Running faster won't always get you further. Which brings me to the second law, Voluntary Attrition.

Earlier, when I was introducing client-centered marketing, I told you about an advisor with eight hundred clients (and no life), whom we helped thin his roster to three hundred clients who actually brought him more revenue. I want to return to him for a moment. In keeping with the Pareto Principle, eighty percent of his original business came from twenty percent of his clients. And about twenty percent of his business came from eighty percent of his clients. The advisor's error in judgment was that he was spending time with the eighty percent at the expense of the twenty percent, clients who were the engine of his business. Furthermore, he was only realizing about fifteen percent of his new clients via referrals. He was also only investing about twenty percent of his overall marketing budget in his clients. The rest was spent on prospecting, on trying to convince new people. The flaw in this approach was that over time, his infrastructure became so huge that in essence he was building a monument to himself.

A Landmark Decision

We next suggested that he take a good look at the eighty percent of his clients who were not the engine of his business and decide who he would be better off without. This took some convincing since his ego drove him to focus only on assets, income and the number of clients he had.

You have to ensure that your existing clients fit your Ideal Client Profile. Obviously, if your best client refers to you his daughter, whose portfolio is $20,000, you're going to bring her on as a client. I also realize that some lower-calibre clients have the ability to refer high-calibre clients on occasion. But discipline yourself to attract only people who fit your profile. Every once in a while you might have to tell someone that, "I'm not the advisor for you, but I can recommend someone who is." You could be doing yourself a huge disservice by not turning those prospects away. Work with the best and target the best, both for what it gets you and for what it makes of you.

Get Serious – Narrow Your Focus

When it comes to pure prospecting, two approaches are open to you: *broadcasting* and *narrowcasting*. Broadcasting is "Here I am" or institutional advertising, such as newspaper ads, radio commercials, billboard signs, junk mail and so on. I refer to this type of marketing as 'spray and pray.' Throw enough mud against the barn door and some of it is sure to stick. As you can probably guess, I rarely endorse broadcasting for an advisor. It's fine for large firms which need to maintain name recognition among their clients and shareholders. But for individual advisors, the best prospecting approach is narrowcasting.

Narrowcasting is when you select two, three or four good geographic or demographic target markets and zoom in on them with laser beam precision, turning them upside down over time. Broadcasting is like the sun, shining on everything. Narrowcasting is like the sun through a magnifying glass. It has the same power, only it has become so harnessed and concentrated on a small area that it has the intensity to burn paper.

You Can't Be Good At Everything

To expand upon these approaches, there are also two types of marketers when it comes to prospecting: specialists and generalists. I can easily determine who is a generalist by looking at their prospect list. A generalist has a prospect list of about three hundred people from at least thirty different walks of life. There has been no methodical approach to assembling the list. Trying to be all things to all people, the advisor ultimately becomes a wandering generality. While I've known advisors who have still achieved well even though they've been haphazardly all over the map, the problem is that they almost certainly never enjoy the benefits of critical mass momentum.

Critical mass is the most elusive goal in marketing. It's achieved when your marketing efforts and disciplines start to take on a life of their own. It's like compound interest. We all know the magic of compounding and the Rule of 72. Unfortunately, generalists never get to experience that feeling of turning the corner because their approach is too fragmented. To play off the old phrase: if you chase too many rabbits, they'll all elude you.

A specialist is someone who realizes that there are only twenty-four hours in the day and only so many people that they will be able to reach. Rather than trying to be all things to all people, they narrow their focus to just a few targets. This is an important step in creating your USP.

If you look at mass marketers, you see that they too are becoming increasingly more focused. For example, a department store by the name of Interstate woke up to the fact that their only profitable department was the toy section. So they became Toys R Us. Volvo's USP is safety. Even when you check out their web site, they advise you to "surf safely."

On The Verge Of A Breakthrough

How does a financial advisor narrowcast and become a specialist? Once again, look at the momentum you already have going for you. Where do your best clients live and what do your best clients do? Perhaps you a have a cluster of clients who live in an affluent neighborhood. The other residents of that community would make a great geographic target market. Maybe your best client is an optometrist. Why not make optometrists a demographic prospect target marketing pillar?

I've seen advisors develop prospecting pillars that include everything from farmers to pharmacists. Some target dentists and orthodontists, others engineers and architects. Many are starting to follow Tom Stanley's advice in *The Millionaire Next Door* by targeting owners of printing companies, car dealerships, furniture stores, pest control companies, bowling allies and so on.

What you also want to do is focus on target markets where you have inside champions, those people who think highly of you, have influence over others and will go to bat for you.

A new financial advisor was trying break out of a rut he'd fallen into. After approaching and bringing on several of his friends and family members as clients, he found his business had stalled. I asked him who he felt could be an inside champion. He thought of a friend, the department head of a high tech company who, although not yet a client, was certain soon to become one. I suggested that the advisor approach him with the following proposition: the advisor would come into the department during lunch, bringing sandwiches and beverages, and he would conduct a lunch-and-learn financial seminar. All he asked his friend to do was poll his staff as to who would be interested. Fourteen people attended, and the advisor generated a few clients. Today, after much refinement, the advisor's most productive prospecting pillar is doing optional, in-house financial lunch-and-learn seminars for companies, all of which got started with the help of the inside champion.

Another advisor developed a pillar of dentists. His wife was a hygienist, and his first dental client was her boss. Today, after an intensive target marketing campaign, he has close to one hundred dentists as part of his inner circle of four hundred clients. (And it's been years since his last cavity.)

We Are In The Specialist Era

Once you have selected target markets based on your inside champions, I want you to take the concept of 'specialist' to another level. Study that target market. Learn it thoroughly. One way you can do this is to ask your inside champion for help.

My favourite example of this is the advisor who asked one of his best clients, a chiropractor, to lunch so that he could pick his brain about bringing value to other chiropractors. His client brought more than his appetite to the table. He brought a directory of other chiropractors in the area and proceeded to check off the ones he knew well. He gave the advisor several copies of chiropractic trade magazines so that the advisor could familiarize himself with the business. He told the advisor which websites he should visit on the Internet. He even invited the advisor to have any of the chiropractors call him for a personal endorsement. Talk about an inside champion! One of the advisor's most important pillars today is that of chiropractors, and he is on the verge of a critical-mass breakthrough.

The advisor has created what is called an 'insider's reputation,' which simply means that over time, chiropractors begin to perceive him as a specialist and the 'go-to' person in their sector. You can further bolster your insider's reputation by being visible within the geo/demo targets you have selected. Write articles in their trade magazines and attend their functions.

As a specialist, you can take your insider's reputation to an even higher level by ensuring that all of your correspondence "speaks directly to the target." What does that mean? Your letters to a chiropractor, for example, must have a chiropractic flavor. By using trade jargon and drawing references to your awareness of the field, you immediately position yourself as "The Man (or Woman) on the Mountain."

What you have to remember is that when a prospect peruses your letter, they either connect with it and say to themselves "me too" or they dismiss outright by saying "so what?" One advisor with four different prospecting pillars has his newsletter customized for each of the four. Eighty percent of each newsletter is identical. The other twenty percent is customized with industry-specific value-adds. Another advisor, who targets lawyers, provides tips on how to use the PC Law software program in his newsletters. Another advisor, who targets human resource professionals, includes tips on team building and boosting morale in his letters to those prospects. He also includes quotes by industry experts, such as the following one by HR guru Robert Half: "There is something that is much more scarce, something rarer than ability. It is the ability to recognize ability." Your letters have to speak specifically to the individual in terms he or she can relate to, not to a stadium filled with people from different walks of life.

Be Visible

If you target geographic communities, be visible at various events and functions. Take the city councilor out for lunch and find out what plans city hall has for the neighborhood. Pass along your observations in letters to the residents on your prospect list.

There is an important caveat to this approach. You have to be patient and maintain faith that what you are doing is being noticed. I've seen advisors "try" narrowcasting, only to get discouraged because it didn't lead to instant gratification. When you abandon a haphazard, wide-angle approach and narrow your prospecting efforts, it doesn't mean the flood gates will instantly open, lavishing you with clients. A narrow focus must be complemented with a long-term view.

You don't have to be too linear in selecting your targets. The obvious geographic and demographic markets that I've mentioned thus far can work well. And I've seen advisors focus on other commonalties, everything from BMW motorcycle owners to aviation buffs to mountain bikers to fly fishing enthusiasts. You can acquire mailing lists to create a customized campaign for virtually every target audience imaginable.

One advisor, an executive MBA grad, started prospecting people who appeared in executive MBA newspaper graduation announcements and has gone on to make it a very lucrative pillar. Another advisor, who wanted to target business owners and retirees, found that many of her teacher clients were married to entrepreneurs. She also found that her clients' parents would be great prospects too. A woman, who once worked in a bank, now does what is called 'geographic farming,' targeting residents of the neighborhood in and around the bank where she worked for seven years. Another advisor, who targeted business owners, would call a prospect and ask if he could buy an hour of that person's time. He said that he wanted to learn all he could about the prospect's business so that he could calibrate his approach to the specific needs of entrepreneurs. Those who accepted his invitation declined the offer of money or simply asked that the advisor donate it to a charity. It has become a major prospecting technique.

I've seen or read about countless marketers who have realized the power of promoting a USP and focusing on specific target markets. A plastic surgeon in Beverly Hills started getting more and more referrals from clients who were flight attendants with major airlines. In an attempt to raise the level of his business, he purchased a mailing list of flight attendants and created an entire campaign directed at them. He talked about the fact that the poor air in airplanes, odd working hours and other stresses led to premature aging lines that could easily be remedied. He included testimonials from satisfied attendant clients and offered free first-class hotel accommodation to those who flew in from out-of-town. He reminded them that because of their airline passes, they could easily fly in to meet him from across the continent for just a few dollars. It was an incredibly successful campaign that created his most lucrative prospecting pillar.

Wherever you have an interest and/or an inside champion, you can make it a pillar. A combination of homework and hard work can lead you to some remarkable rewards.

Getting Busy

Once you have selected your three or four prospecting pillars, you will be anxious to start. This is understandable. Just before we talk technique, however, let's first gain clarity about your immediate goals regarding your prospects. You might be thinking, "Goals? I know what my goals are. I want to convert them to clients." Fair enough, but there are a few steps that first serve as a prelude. Getting a client is a desired result. Based on the Law of Cause and Effect, we have to take a microscope to the reasons that lead to the desired result.

Your first prospecting objective is to sift the true prospects from the suspects and begin the process of positioning yourself in their minds as Number Two. All of the people you will be prospecting are already dealing with someone else. Whether it's a banker, financial planner or investment advisor, the prospect has his or her money elsewhere. You want to position yourself as the next in line, using what is called the contrast principle. In your case, the contrast principle says that the moment a prospect perceives you as being more attractive than his or her current advisor, only then will that person consider moving to you. Also, the moment the prospect's current advisor drops the ball dramatically, odds increase that he or she will go to Number Two.

Your prospecting efforts have to create a nagging feeling in the minds of your prospects that they are with the wrong person and should move. You have to arouse concern in their minds that builds dissatisfaction with their current situation. This practice occurs in mass marketing all the time. A soap company, paper towel company or deodorant company will show how great its product is, comparing it to the performance of a leading competitor. Essentially, they are saying, "If you are using the other company's product, look at what you are missing. If you are already using ours, don't even think about switching."

You often see a Coca-Cola vending machine in front of a Wal-Mart store. It sells a can of Coke for the impossibly low price of thirty-five cents rather than the normal price of a dollar. What they hope you perceive is that if Wal-Mart can sell its Coke for thirty-five cents, *all* of its store prices must be low as well.

A group of resorts in Stowe, Vermont carried out an advertising campaign called "The Top 10 Ski Resorts in the World" targeted to people who lived on the Eastern seaboard of the United States. The ad photographically listed ski locations in Europe, Colorado and British Columbia, and toward the bottom was listed Stowe, with the caption, "The only difference is that you can drive to our resorts."

The contrast principle is persuasive because it compares what you already know with what's also available. If your prospects feel they would get better value from you than from their current advisor, they might say to themselves, "I don't even know this person. Imagine how well I'd be treated if I were a client." Since many advisors unwittingly neglect their clients, achieving contrast is easier than you might think.

How To Win Them Over

You have to decide now how you are going to win your prospects to come onside. A wide variety of prospecting vehicles, such as seminars, trade shows, cold calls, advertising and direct mail, is available to you. You already know my position on broadcast marketing. With few exceptions, there is little need for an advisor to do any of it. You know where I stand on cold calling. Don't get me wrong, however; the phone is an incredible prospecting tool. My contention is that it be used to augment your other marketing efforts, especially my personal favorite, direct mail.

Of all the marketing methodologies, a postage stamp is still the least intrusive yet most efficient and professional available to you. There are some things you need to know, however. While the mail is powerful, we now get exposed to more mail in one day than we did in an entire week just ten years ago. As a result, people have become indifferent to much of the unsolicited information they receive by post, and they sort their mail over a garbage can. If your mail isn't distinctive, you might as well throw it in your own garbage can and save the stamps. You must do certain things in order to wipe away the apathetic fog most people are in when they read their mail. You need to rely on proven strategies to create a response.

Get It There

For starters, get a good list of prospects. You might be able to craft the world's greatest letters, but if they are going to a bunch of dead-beat suspects, the results will be miserable. Directories and mailing lists are available for virtually every geographic and demographic target market you can imagine. From new home-owners in a specific neighborhood to the subscribers of mountain bike magazine, data on virtually everyone is bought and sold everyday. If you are targeting business owners and you want to keep your costs down, grab the yellow pages and call the firms listed there to get the names and full addresses from the receptionists. (If you are grilled on your intentions, tell them that you need to forward the owner important time-sensitive financial information.) Give yourself a week or so to compile the list; make it comprehensive.

If you want to be a little more adventurous, contact a mailing list broker and explain what you are looking for. They will rent or sell a list of virtually any sector. You can buy reverse residential directories (a directory listing street addresses first, followed by names and phone numbers) or visit the reference section of your local library. City Hall can also be quite helpful, as can the Internet. Whatever you use, secure a good list.

Get Your Letter Opened And Read

As I mentioned, people receive an incredible amount of mail, most of it of no interest to them. There isn't a lot you can do with the outside of the envelope to dress it up. Various non-financial marketers stamp their envelopes with 'urgent' messages and other attention-getters. All I recommend is that you neatly handwrite the address on each envelope. Since I only suggest sending small batches of correspondence at any given time, this can physically be done. Other than that, when it comes to the envelope, keep it simple and understated. Depending on the nature of the offer, you might occasionally write "personal and confidential" at the bottom left and offset it with a highlighting pen.

I also recommend that you consider using a variety of envelope sizes in your sequence of mailings to prospects. This removes the mass mailing feel that regular envelopes impart. It will also create intrigue. If you choose not to hand-write the name and address, have it printed directly on the envelope rather than using labels. It takes more time but it's worth it. Finally, use a unique font.

As for the contents, your first concern is the hook, that feature of the letter that grabs the prospect's attention. There are two primary types of hooks – *phraseology headlines* at the top of your letter and *lumpy inserts*.

A phraseology headline conveys a benefit or presents a problem with which the prospect can relate. Again, it's a matter soliciting the "Me too" response or the "So what?" dismissal. If the headline isn't effective, the rest of the letter isn't important because it won't be read anyway.

Let me give a few non-financial examples. I saw an advertisement in a Spanish magazine for a washing machine. The headline read, "Mas tiempo por amor," which, when translated into English means, "More time for love." That is a classic "me too" promise statement that conveys a specific benefit. Another ad in a trade magazine for restaurant owners promoted a new kind of french fry. The headline read, "Don't let soggy fries dampen your profits." (And you thought you had business problems.) That is a "me too" problem with which restaurant owners can identify. The beauty of presenting a problem is that it arouses dissatisfaction in the prospect's mind and asks that he or she focus on solutions – hopefully the solutions you offer.

Here are a couple of basic headlines:

• "Are your Investments Achieving Peak Performance?"

- "Will the Tax Department be the Primary Beneficiary of your Estate?"
- "Well-Kept Investment Secrets All Investors Should Know."
- "The Top Ten Reasons Why Our Investment Kit Can Help You."
- "Honey, I Shrunk My Tax Bill."

Quotes also work well as headlines for letters. Link your quote to the theme of your letter so that it is meaningful to the target reader. A couple of good examples might be:

- "Rule #1: Never lose money. Rule #2: Never forget the first rule."
  - Warren Buffett

- "Facts don't cease to exist because they are ignored."
  - Aldous Huxley

- "Wealth is the product of man's capacity to think."
  - Ayn Rand

- "If there is a better way to do something, find it."
  - Thomas Edison

- "Nurture great thoughts, for you will never go higher than your thoughts."
  - Benjamin Disraeli

- "Allow myself to introduce…myself."
  - Austin Powers (Just kidding)

Differentiating with Lumpy Mail

With respect to lumpy mail hooks, I personally like them. The concept falls under the category of multi-sensory marketing – marketing hooks that appeal to the various senses. It happens all around us. When you have an open house, the realtor asks that you bake bread or muffins to create a down-home atmosphere. When Lexus introduced their new GS sports car, the promotional brochure that was inserted into newspapers was intentionally scented with the aroma of a leather car interior. Lumpy mail appeals to the touch sense.

One advisor carried out a small letter campaign to business owners. The phraseology headline read, "Is the Tax Department Giving You a Headache?" To add a little sizzle, he glued a small tin of Anacin to each letter. In smaller font under the headline ran the phrase, "You can take two of these or call me. But I last longer." When he followed up the mailer, he told the receptionists that he was the guy who had sent the Anacin. Most of them had found it quite funny, and in most cases he spoke with the owner personally and with good success, I might add.

Another advisor, who was targeting female entrepreneurs, sent a letter inviting them to attend her financial seminar. The headline read, "Brush up on your financial knowledge." She enclosed a toothpaste sample that she received in bulk from her dentist.

As a variation to the golfing tee theme, another advisor, primarily targeting widows and divorcees, used the headline, "Financial Planning to a Tea." Her lumpy enclosure was a tea bag affixed to each letter. Her 'PS' read, "You'll be glad to know that I won't be reading tea leaves to predict your financial future."

While phraseology headlines are the most common, lumpy mail gets the most attention. That's because it's intriguing and it's different. Marketers call this a Point of Difference, or POD for short.

I first learned the power of the POD while reading *Ogilvy on Advertising* by David Ogilvy. He created a magazine ad campaign for Hathaway shirts which featured a model wearing smart and stylish shirts in various exotic locations around the world. Because he felt his ads looked too much like those of his competitors, he dressed the model in a black eye patch. It made the campaign a hit. (I know what you're thinking, but it makes it too hard to read the ANDEX chart.)

People get pounded with so much marketing information that they have become skeptical, apathetic and numb to most of what's out there. Instead of using copy-cat marketing that often goes unnoticed, my advice to compensate for this is that you differentiate.

I realize that some people think lumpy mail is hokey, and in some cases they're right. It isn't always appropriate. It's a personal call that each advisor makes for him or herself.

Hold Their Attention And Garner A Response

Max Sacheim, the "Little Giant" of direct response marketing, always lived by what he called the "Four Whys" that run through a prospect's mind as he or she considers a marketing piece in their hands:

- Why should I read this?
- Why should I believe it?
- Why should I act on it?
- Why should I act on it *right now*?

These are good questions to use as guidelines when you sculpt your letters.

Teach and Be Topical

I have already mentioned some of the factors necessary to ensure that your marketing pieces are compelling, such as differentiating, being entertaining and using social proof. While I agree that Warren Buffett was bang on about the marketplace wanting to be entertained, I still believe that financial advisors should weave a meaningful amount of interesting and educational information into their marketing, and here's why:

Years ago, during the Industrial Revolution, people made money with their hands through their physical labours. In today's Information Age, we have created a Learning Revolution whereby people make money with their minds. Not since the invention of the printing press back in A.D.1455 have we seen such a renaissance in an individual's ability to learn and power to persuade, via such sources as the Internet and other high tech corridors. Coupled with the fact that we are in an era of personal responsibility, people have come to realize that they can't depend on the company where they work, the government or any other institution to take care of their financial futures. They'll be left by the side of the road if they do. Consequently, people have a voracious appetite for knowledge and for the sense of empowerment that comes with it. If you can satisfy that appetite, you will attract a steady stream of high-calibre people.

Here's another example from David Ogilvy to prove my point. He discovered early on that if a marketing piece teaches something, it creates higher recall, interest, appreciation and reciprocation. Being helpful, therefore, reflects well on you and is a sure-fire way to connect with the people to whom you want to be connected. Ogilvy ran a campaign for Guinness Beer and dedicated almost the entire ad space to informing people about different types of oysters from around the world. Only a small portion of the ad made reference to the fact that Guinness Beer goes well with oysters.

Mitel, an international telecommunications company, ran a campaign celebrating their 25th anniversary. The ad took readers down memory lane, reminding them of what had taken place in the world during each year since the company's inception. It spurred interest and provoked thought, just as it was meant to do.

Use Proper Phraseology

An important component in creating a good "me too" letter is your choice of language throughout it. For example, think of the words 'life insurance.' It truly is *death* insurance, but we both know why it's called what it is. I could describe the hallway in Toronto's Royal York Hotel as one hundred and ten yards long, or I could tell you it's as long as a football field. Which imparts length better? It's all in the way we say things that makes them have impact.

Using sound bites is one of the most effective ways to grab attention and become memorable. In films, we hear them all the time: "Show me the money," "Go ahead, make my day," and "Alrighty then." They are intentional devices, repeated at opportune moments, to reinforce a concept in a stylish manner so that people will adopt them and plug the movie.

The following sound bites are portions of phrases that you should incorporate into your letters to build persuasiveness. Modify them according to your needs:

- You might be saying to yourself…
- Don't you owe it to yourself…
- Every once in a while, an opportunity comes along that redefines…

- As you can imagine...
- That said...
- As you can imagine, a commonly asked question by investors is...
- You'll be glad to know that the people who have used this approach are...
- The second best investment idea is...
- My family laughed when I told them I was going to be financially independent...
- Have you ever wished that investing could be...
- If you are like most entrepreneurs I speak with, you are looking for...
- As a financial advisor who works closely with (target), I take great pride in...
- Let's face it, as a (target) you get approached all the time by advisors who...
- It's hard to argue with the exhaustive studies that have proven this concept...
- Right up front, as a (target) you know all about the importance of...
- I can relate because many of my clients are (target)...
- What steps have you taken to insulate yourself from...
- There couldn't be a better time to take advantage of...
- As a (target) you undoubtedly want the peace of mind that comes with...
- A clear indicator of a sound financial plan is...
- Because you are a (target), I am inviting you to...
- A wide range of choice and a full array of services are crucial to...

Use the Right Format

Envision the flow of a letter as water flowing through a funnel, starting out wide and compressing as it narrows. This feature is one of the first things I look for in letters I critique.

When studying the structure of the letter, I use what is called the AICA formula. Regardless of its length, the letter must have four basic sections, each of which is represented by the letters in the AICA acronym.

Right off the top, the first section of the letter must grab the reader's *attention*, with a headline that conveys a benefit. But the reader is still standing over the garbage can. It's now critical to hold *interest*. Next, you have to build *confidence* so that the reader will ultimately *act*.

Often, a good AICA letter will also incorporate what is called PAS, which stands for Problem/Agitate/Solve. Some of the best attention-getting headlines are problems with which the prospect can connect. The best way to hold interest is to agitate the problem you have presented. Do this by expanding upon the problem. The final step is to present a solution for the problem you have just agitated.

Here's a basic example. Let's assume you were a prospect on a list I had acquired of affluent people in a wealthy neighborhood loaded with ideal estate-planning candidates. Let's examine a way to blend both the AICA and PAS formulas.

The headline would read, "The 7 Most Common Estate-Planning Mistakes and How to Avoid Them." This *problem* statement should get your *attention* because you don't want to make any of those mistakes. Curious, you read on. "It has been proven that 51% of people will inadvertently make the tax department the number one beneficiary of their estate once everything has been transferred." I have just held your *interest* by *agitating* the potential problem. After agitating a little more, I would build your *confidence* and lead you to *action* with my solution.

"As Estate Planning professionals, working with many residents in Woodland Heights, we have prepared an informative report outlining the seven most common estate-planning mistakes and ways to avoid them. If you feel this report would be helpful, call us at your convenience, and we will forward one to you with our compliments."

You could add a 'PS' to head off any "What's the catch?" objections. "PS. You might be asking yourself why we would offer these reports for free. We take great pride in helping people make informed decisions about their personal estate-planning needs. Everyone's situation is unique, and we feel that armed with the right game plan, people can move forward confidently. As you can imagine, these reports are very popular. If you see value in the information and you would like us to examine your current plan, we'd be delighted to do so."

Use The Dual Readership Path

You next need to consider the overall appearance of your letter. I strongly recommend a format called the *dual readership path*. Its origins stem from magazines. Editors realized that people don't just grab a magazine off the shelf and start reading an article word-for-word; they peruse it first and take snapshots of the articles in search of something that appeals to them.

If you look at magazines such as *Esquire* or *Vanity Fair*, you'll notice that each article has a headline accompanied by pictures of the subject. Throughout the text of the article, you will find woven throughout what are called "pull quotes," bolded quotations and statements sprinkled among the smaller text that serve to grab people's attentions as they scan and flip. Typically, a prospective customer will pluck the magazine from the shelf, flip through it, connect with an article that intrigues them, take a snapshot of the article and decide at that point if they're going to buy the magazine.

Your letters work much the same way. A prospect will open the envelope and glance at the letter. In scanning it, the prospect will immediately take in your headline and the bolded statements that you've placed between the paragraphs of text. If you have done a good job, your prospect's internal dialogue begins to embrace the rest of the letter.

The dual readership path is additionally effective because it appeals to both the left- and right-brain prospect. Left-brain folk are more analytical and detail-oriented. These people follow instructions step-by-step when assembling a stereo cabinet. Right-brain people are more visual and big picture-oriented. They would attempt to assemble that same cabinet by simply looking at the picture on the outside of the packaging that it came in. If you are a left-brain person and you write a left-brain letter, guess who won't read it? Exactly, right-brain and vice versa.

Moreover, the dual readership path prevents you from rambling on with a long-winded feature dump. It makes the letter more punchy and helps you get to the point faster. I'm not suggesting that you can't write a three or four-page letter. The length of the letter is not the issue. The issue is whether or not the letter is engaging or boring. Busy people, the very people you are trying to target, read what interests them, regardless of its length. However, brevity is still a factor, and I remain partial to a snappy one-page letter that utilizes the dual readership path format.

Finish Strong

"Telling isn't selling." That expression is one of my favourite in marketing. I know a lot of advisors who are skilled at presenting their message in a variety of ways but not at persuading. Why? Because of a weak *call-to-action*. The call-to-action tells a person what it is you want them to do. A shampoo company, for example, increases sales by thirty percent with the addition of a simple call-to-action on the back of the bottle of shampoo. After instructing customers on how to use the product, they add one word – "repeat" – and consumption increases thirty percent.

A restaurant in a funky part of town displays a neon sign in their window that reads, "Get in here." Sure enough, the place is packed. FedEx erects a huge billboard that simply reads, "FedEx," a simple institutional "Here-I-am" advertisement. They change the sign to read *www.fedex.com*. It has now become a call-to-action asking that people log on to their website.

Your letters must always end with a call-to-action. You have to ask prospects to do something. The challenge you face is that the products and services you sell are quite abstract and intangible. You are selling the promise of the future and a relationship. Therefore, your calls-to-action are that much more important. They also position you as a marketer rather than a salesperson – and there is a distinction.

Here is a basic outline for creating your calls-to-action:

• Ask prospects to do something. Avoid the passive "Here I am" letters that introduce you but do little else than serve as glorified business cards.

• Give prospects a reason to do something. The reason has to be perceived as a tremendous benefit and that they would be doing themselves a considerable disservice by not acting.

- Make it easy for them to do something. Your call-to-action must radiate trust and be non-threatening and disarming.

- Make them want to do something *right now*. You are trying to create a sense of urgency, using an alluring incentive or gentle fear-of-loss.

The best call-to-action is one that provides a valid or tangible benefit rather than an abstract one. A men's clothing store would be far better off advertising a sport jacket sale by saying, "Buy a sport jacket and receive a free pair of dress slacks." It is far better than saying, "All sport jackets 30% off." A customer can visualize a pair of pants, but they are skeptical about the validity of a so-called "sale."

Let me give you another example. While flipping through the local newspaper, I happened upon a full-page ad promoting Walt Disney World. It was very compelling. As I read it, I thought, "What are they going to ask me to do?" I was certain that they would tell me to call a travel agent or Disney World directly to book my vacation. Never once did they do that. Instead, their call-to-action read, "Call now to receive an exciting travel planning video." They converted the abstract of spending several thousand dollars on a vacation to something very tangible, a video. They also made it non-threatening and easy.

In another example, I watched a television commercial for Quicken software. It was punchy and informative. Again, I found myself wondering what the call-to-action would be. Call a toll-free number to order their software over the phone? Visit a software store and buy the product? Wrong again. They asked me to call for a free demo diskette in order to learn all of the benefits of Quicken in the comfort of my own home. Again, it was easy, non-threatening and compelling.

Give Prospects A Bridge To Cross

In both of those cases, Disney and Quicken used what is called a *bridge*, a no-obligation, tangible call-to-action that helps serve in making a prospect into a customer. I'm not suggesting that everyone who orders a video or diskette will buy something. But that's not the point of a bridge. It is designed to make the phone ring. Both Disney and Quicken could have run basic "Here I am" ads that told people to go to Disney World or simply buy Quicken, but most people would have simply passed them by.

Here now is a financial example:

An advisor asked me to review a letter that he had mailed to three hundred prospects. It was a well-written letter to promote a health care fund, citing demographic shifts and other logical reasons why it made sense to invest in that sector. He had even screened a pie chart over the text for visual enhancement. Problem was, no one responded. His call-to-action read, "Call me to discuss this exciting fund." It wasn't exactly something to prompt people to jump on the phone. He was dejected when I pointed out his mistake, but I told him it was a good start and that it built a level of familiarity with the product among his prospects. So we sent the same three hundred people another letter four weeks later.

That letter started, "Hi again. A couple of weeks ago, I sent you a letter detailing an exciting health care mutual fund. I haven't heard from you yet. I can only assume that you've been simply too busy and haven't had a chance to respond. The feedback we've received has been unbelievable." (We took some liberties; in my view, zero was unbelievable – unbelievably bad – but we didn't embellish.)

Here was our call-to-action: "So what I've decided to do is create an informative investment kit to describe this exciting fund. In this kit is an audiocassette for you to listen to in the privacy of your car, as well as helpful reports and articles about demographic shifts and other reasons which make this fund such a tremendous opportunity.

"As you can imagine [being assumptive], these kits are very popular [social proof], and I don't have many of them [fear of loss]. If you feel it would help you make an informed decision [teach and be topical], call me immediately [sense of urgency], and I'll send one to you with my compliments [non-threatening bridge]."

Within five days, the advisor had more than thirty people call him for the kit. I'm not suggesting they all became clients. You can't mistake their intent for consent. But that wasn't the point. I wanted the advisor to sift out key prospects who were hovering on the verge of a decision from the rest of the prospects, to give them a reason to call. It's still the advisor's job to cross the bridge and convert each prospect into becoming a customer. A great bonus was that the fund company provided all of the material.

Create Intellectual Properties

Create several intellectual properties and use them as part of your calls-to-action. Put together special kits. Use various reports to lure a response. Give prospects something to act upon. Dupont ran a campaign in magazines to promote their new virtually indestructible Tyvek paper fabric (used for courier envelopes and the like). The headline read, "Go ahead, try to tear me." The ad was printed on the actual paper, which was fastened into the magazine. It was expensive, but what powerful testimony!

The Ottawa Senators Hockey Team carried out a mail campaign to promote season's ticket packages of six or twelve tickets. The campaign was, "Let's put our stamp on the NHL." Enclosed was a sheet of stamps featuring all the logos of other teams in the NHL. Readers were asked to lick and stick the stamps of the teams they wanted to see and mail back their orders.

Your audio newsletter and/or printed piece would make for a good prospect call-to-action.

You can send a Peak Performance Checklist with your prospecting letters that says, "Is your current financial advisor helping you to achieve Peak Performance?" The checklist identifies all of the value-added services you offer, be they a fax-on-demand system, regular seminars, a lending library or whatever. The checklist asks prospects to compare their current advisors' services to yours. It gets them involved and gives you something to point to in future conversations.

You can send prospects an investment report card that they can fill out and return to you to evaluate their progress and overall invest-ment strategies (not to mention the advice of their current advisors). You can send them a certificate that offers a "One-hour personalized financial needs analysis." The certificate should state a perceived dollar value as well as a response deadline. The prospect is asked to complete the information on the certificate and fax it back to you.

Furthermore, it's always a good idea to focus on what is called *pre-disposed lead acquisition*. This term simply means that you are dividing your prospect list into two sections, prime prospects and regular prospects. Your best prospecting asset will be your list of prime prospects. These people are defined by the simple criteria that they have called you in response to an offer whereas the others haven't.

Sift The Prime Prospects

Let me illustrate this concept using the Disney and Quicken examples. If ten thousand people saw the Disney ad in the newspaper, Disney achieved good exposure and name recognition within that group. But if six hundred of the ten thousand people called Disney for the free video, those six hundred would be considered prime prospects. Why? Because, they called Disney – they placed an inbound call. Disney now owns those six hundred names (their predisposed lead acquisitions). Chances are good that those six hundred people are going to be receiving correspondence from Disney for years to come. When a movie comes out on video, those six hundred will be among the first to know about it.

Let's take it one step further. Are those six hundred people more likely to go to Disney World after watching that tape? By adding the bridge, Disney has without question put the odds in its own favour.

It works the same way with the people who responded to the free Quicken demo diskette offer. Those people don't feel threatened by the offer. They requested the diskette and will use it once it arrives. Familiarity for the product is enhanced, and the likelihood that those people will eventually buy skyrockets.

A publishing company runs an ad for a new novel by a well-known author. At the bottom of the ad is a small coupon that reads, "If you buy this book before the end of the month, send in your receipt with this coupon and you'll receive a two-dollar rebate." For two dollars a head, the publishing company is essentially buying names. They will sell that list to other companies wishing to target that demographic, and they will build a good prospect list for future target marketing campaigns when new books are launched.

You buy a new coffeemaker and receive a five-dollar mail-in rebate. You send it in and receive your cheque. You have just sold your name for five dollars. You now fit into a demographic sector which will be used in future campaigns.

Everything from contest entry forms, special shopping clubs, frequent flyer air miles programs and other loyalty reward programs are primarily offered to gather names and to buy patterns and other important data while further insulating the buyer from competitive influences.

Prospecting In Action
Let me give you a few more examples of how the contrast principle, lead acquisition and bridges can be used in your business.

A financial advisor decides to target business people, using fly fishing as a hook (no pun intended). He partners with the owner of a fishing store. They collaborate by doing a dinner event called, "Fishing for Better Returns." The advisor does a financial state-of-the-nation and passes along investment ideas. The owner of the fishing store gives a presentation of fishing tactics and tricks. Both get good exposure in front of a captive audience. The store owner lends his list of two thousand customers to the advisor, allowing the advisor to send the letters of invitation to the event. The letter is structured so that those who can't attend can order a free investment kit. Ninety people respond, forty to attend the seminar and fifty to receive the kit. The fifty who order the kit have in actual fact said, "I'm interested in knowing more about you..." The advisor now owns those fifty names. At the seminar, he meets the forty prospects. He can follow up with them and hopefully be able to convert some of them into clients. When he returns the list of two thousand fishing store customers, the advisor has an asset of ninety new prospects.

Another advisor runs a retirement lifestyle symposium, featuring a speaker who talks about the lifestyle aspects of retirement. He invites his clients to bring along a friend. He involves promotional partners and encourages them to use the event for their clients. He targets a neighborhood of about five hundred homes which has a high concentration of retired people or those on the verge of retiring. Fifty of the five hundred respond to the offer to attend, which frankly aren't bad numbers. However, why would 450 people decide not to attend? Are they tired of seminars? Were they out of town? So the advisor records the seminar and has five hundred audio tapes produced. He then sends each of the 450 people who didn't attend a letter that reads, "Did You Miss It?" across the top. The letter continues: "A couple of weeks ago, we invited you to seminar that you were unfortunately unable to attend. The seminar was a big hit, and a number of people have asked if I will be offering another. I have the next best thing. We recorded the event and now have audiocassettes available. If you wish you could have been there, call us and we'll forward the cassette to you with our compliments." Close to fifty people called for the cassette on the first invitation. This is a good example of sifting and lead acquisition in action.

The advisor also asked the people attending the seminar if they knew a friend who would have liked to have heard it to call for a cassette at no charge. Within six months of the event, advisor had given out over five hundred cassettes. His clients loved them, and it was an incredible way to build a good prospect list and to follow up client conversions.

Tangible intellectual properties serve as good ice breakers when you follow up with those who order them. They also give you something to discuss should you choose to follow up with those who don't order them. Such was the case with the advisor who promoted the health care fund to the three hundred prospects mentioned earlier.

Know When To Use A Bridge
Having said all of that, I'm not suggesting that bridges are universally suited to all prospecting situations, nor am I suggesting that they will always work. I am suggesting, however, that they will

increase the likelihood of generating more inbound calls. Again, you are putting the ball in the prospect's court and asking that he or she hit it back. But remember, you can't want your prospects to become clients more than they do. Make them work for it.

Whatever you do, don't let prospects off the hook when you approach them through the mail. Your call-to-action should never read, "I'll be following up with you in a few weeks to discuss this with you." You are essentially saying to them, "Don't worry, I'll do all the work." If you are going to follow up on the phone – and I encourage you to – don't warn them ahead of time.

There are a couple of other things to keep in mind. Tell your prospects who it is and what it is you want to attract. If your new client entry level is a portfolio in excess of one hundred thousand dollars, tell prospects in your letters to them. Mention that the information you provide and the knowledge you have refined is ideally suited for people with an investment portfolio exceeding one hundred thousand dollars. (How convenient.)

I also recommend that you occasionally add a diplomatic *take-back close* in your letters. This technique, which essentially tests a prospect's real interest in you, makes a bold statement about both your code of conduct and about the kind of clients with whom you work. It is usually added at the end of your call-to-action. For example, you might say, "If you are looking for an advisor who will hound you all the time, urging you to act on every so-called "hot stock" tip, then I'm not the advisor for you. If you are looking for an advisor who uses a conservative, time-tested approach to investments, then I am most certainly your advisor of choice."

Additional Points to Consider

When sculpting your letters, here are a few additional tips:

- Start every letter with what is called a 'drop down' letter, in which the first letter of the first word of the first paragraph is larger than the rest.

- Ensure that the opening paragraph is brief and catchy. If you read an article in a good magazine or newspaper, the opening paragraph is generally written to draw the reader into the story.

- Be specific. Avoid using generalities or abstracts. Denominate, define and quantify as often as possible.

- Clearly explain benefits. Whenever you introduce a feature of a product or service, or whenever you make a promise statement, elaborate. Use examples and expand upon them with transitional ties that begin, "What this means to you is..." The improved french fry example mentioned earlier in the book had the phraseology headline, "Don't let Soggy Fries Dampen Your Profits." The new french fry with the clear batter apparently held in heat longer and thus extended the time it took before the fry became cold and soggy. The benefit of the product was, "extended holding time," a feature restauranteurs could surely understand. The ad explained the benefit, stating, "Clear battered fries lock in the heat and fresh taste, delaying the deterioration process longer. That means less waste, better taste and more profitability for you without dampening customer satisfaction."

- Be conversational in your letters. Always write them as if you were writing to a good friend. Keep in mind that "Facts tell, stories sell." People always connect more favourably with a story that stimulates their imaginations and helps them visualize the information that they are reading.

- Be careful using metaphors, analogies and stories. Sometimes, in an attempt to be creative, the real issue can be lost. Take, for example, the television commercial coffee campaign which featured a man and woman in a series of increasingly romantic exchanges. Each episode added a snippet to the story of their growing attraction to each other. It was a memorable campaign. The problem was, most people connected with the story and the characters who were portrayed; when surveyed, however, they couldn't remember the name of the coffee company.

Four Marketing "Don'ts"
- Don't preach. Some letters are very heavy-handed and come off

sounding condescending or preachy. It's a sure recipe for a brutally low response.

- Don't feature dump. Elaborate on key points and whet readers' appetites, but always leave them wanting more.

- Don't 'spray and pray.' It's easy to mistake movement for achievement. Just because you are sending a lot of mail doesn't mean that it is having an impact. Select your targets diligently and take a less-is-more approach.

- Don't bail out. Former British Prime Minister Margaret Thatcher often said, "It's easy to be a starter, but are you a sticker too? It's easy enough to begin a job, it's harder to see it through." If I had ten seconds to present a seminar on prospecting, I'd simply read that quotation to the audience and leave the room (after my opening joke, of course). It defines what separates the best from the rest in virtually every field of endeavour, and it definitely applies to being effective in your business as well.

A few years ago, I attended a conference featuring former U.S. General Norman Schwartzkopf as the keynote speaker. He stated that in battle, one has to find the opposition's weakness and exploit it. He added that the same is true in business. The biggest weakness among one's competitors is their lack of discipline and willingness to finish the job. The best advisors take a long-term view, delay gratification, do the things that are hard and necessary, and finish what they start. The rest want instant gratification and things that are fun and easy to do. They rarely finish the job.

I can't help but be reminded of that time back in 1989 when I was first exposed to Jim Rohn's philosophy. On that little tape I received, Jim asked the question, "Are you today where you said you were going to be five years ago?" When I mentally answered the question, it was with a resounding, "NO!" Jim continued by asking, "If you answered, 'No,' then why not? I know people who set goals and go on to achieve them five years later. What happened to you?" I thought about it but couldn't come up with the answer. He then said, "Get a sheet of paper and a pen, and write down all the things that you feel have held you back." I managed to come up with some items on my list that I felt were legitimately steering me down the wrong path. When I turned the tape back on, Jim told me to look closely at the list. He said that chances are the only thing wrong with my list was that I wasn't on it. He was so right. Everything I had written involved people and circumstances beyond my control. Basically, I was hoping that things would get better. Jim suggested that it wasn't "things" that needed to get better; rather, it was me who needed to improve. I wasn't a victim of circumstances; I was a victim of myself, my own errors in judgment and lack of self-discipline. That experience will stick with me for the rest of my life.

Self-discipline is what separates the best from the rest in the financial services field as well. What's interesting is that everything necessary to achieve a high level of effectiveness is actually easy to do. The problem is that those disciplines are easier not to do. It is easy to put things off. Successful people understand the power of the Law of Diminishing Intent, which simply states that when I get exposed to an idea, knowing that it will impact my life, I should act on it right away. If I don't, chances are I never will. When I put something off, other things start competing for my attention. Before long, my intent to take action diminishes.

Spaced Repetition Is Your Key To Prospecting Success

The best discipline you can develop as it relates to prospecting is a practice called *spaced repetition* marketing. Based on learning theory, it holds that exposure to information over a period of time dramatically improves retention of that information better than one massive bombardment. It makes sense to me. That's how we learn to walk, master a new language, ride a bike, drive a car.

In marketing, the non-technical term for spaced repetition is *linked and sequential dripping*. It is a variation on imprinting. To use a water analogy, if I dumped the entire load of a water truck on your backyard lawn, some would be absorbed but most would either run off or evaporate before it had a chance to sink in. However, if I methodically poured small amounts at a time over a period of time, far more water would be retained. (Either way, I'm sure you'd tell me to get off of your lawn.)

Bill collectors were the first to use spaced-repetition marketing. They would send a letter to a delinquent debtor. If they received no response within a couple of weeks, a second and more urgent letter would be sent. This would continue with a third letter, if necessary. If there was still no response, a phone call would be made. This sequential dripping approach led to a dramatic increase in collections. (Don't ask me why I know this.) Today, several top companies and individual marketers are using linked and sequential drip campaigns with great success.

There are three primary reasons why dripping is so effective. First, it builds familiarity between you and your prospects. People tend to conduct business with people and businesses that are familiar to them, which is why brand names are so important to mass marketers. Some of the most successful companies in their fields don't necessarily sell the best product, but recognition and familiarity have given them an edge.

In addition to building familiarity between you and the prospect, each drip is an investment because it complements your efforts to contrast and position yourself. When you identify a promising prospect and begin the dripping process, you owe it to yourself to see it through.

Thirdly, dripping counters the Law of Diminishing Intent. When a prospect doesn't respond, he or she isn't necessarily saying, "No, " but perhaps instead, "Not now" or "I don't know." The problem is that even though a prospect might look at your letter and think that the offer sounds good, if it isn't acted upon immediately, it will be forgotten. Your subsequent drips breathe life back into the prospect's interest level.

Dripping applies to client marketing as well. You'll recall the financial advisor who sent out the FORM questionnaire to his clients in order to gather information for his profiles. He sent a letter to all of his clients, and to his shocked dismay realized a nine-percent response. He sends a second letter as a reminder three weeks after the first, reiterating the value of the information and including another questionnaire and stamped return envelope. His response rate rose to forty-seven percent.

It's Time to DRIP
The following guideline, in the form of (yet again) another acronym, should help you roll out a spaced repetition marketing campaign.

The D, of course, stands for Discipline. I've seen countless advisors with every credential imaginable, sitting at their desks and wondering why their phones aren't ringing, all because they lack self-discipline. On the other hand, I've seen advisors face countless obstacles yet still manage to achieve greatness because of their tenacity, urgency and commitment to starting and seeing a job through to completion. The rewards don't always go to the person whose oar is in the water first. They often go to those who keep pulling. Every time you go back to a prospect with a valuable drip, you further distance yourself from the other advisors who are vying for that prospect's business.

The R stands for Respect. My best advice is that you lean on a prospect with respect. It is definitely possible to drip on someone annoyingly. You want your prospects to look forward to what you send them, to be at least receptive to your message, which is why you should never use the phone the first time you contact a prospect. Instead, send a professional and informative series of three letters to build familiarity and awareness for your message. Then use the phone for follow-up.

The I stands for Inform. Be respectful by ensuring that all of your drips bring good value to your prospects. The word FORM is woven into the word *inform* and for good reason. It should remind you to diversify your drips. If they involve strictly money issues, it will take that much longer for you to realize a breakthrough, primarily because of an absence of a point of difference. Your drips have to stand out from your competitors.

An advisor working with us decided to hold a Global Investment symposium in which he was featured with several fund company wholesalers to discuss global investment opportunities. The first drip was a traditional invitation on his letterhead which garnered a reasonable response. We suggested that the advisor contact an Asian embassy or consulate to see if they could provide several hundred post cards that he might use for his second drip. The Malaysian consulate pleasantly complied. The response to the postcard reminder was staggering.

So look for opportunities to mix things up a little and create some intrigue. While all drips are valid, those that are truly effective should transcend the obvious letters, e-mail, fax-broadcasts, and so on. Add personality and pick your spots. There is no doubt that FORM information will present greater opportunities for you to add sizzle. If you are speaking with a prospect who casually mentions that she bought a new boat, send a copy of a boating magazine with your next correspondence. Be matter-of-fact about it. Simply note on a post-it, "I saw this in a magazine store and thought of you. I couldn't resist. I really hope you're enjoying your new boat."

Don't be too smarmy with your drips, however. While a creative drip can be your Trojan horse in getting you through the door, you have to be mindful of the overall message you are conveying. You should always have a good reason to drip. Don't send information for the sake of sending it. Persuasion doesn't stem from trying to impress people; it stems from impressing upon them. There really is a difference.

The P in DRIP serves double-duty and stands for Patience and Persistence. In other words, finish the job. As a friend of mine says,

"When it comes to prospecting, you've got to be like a dog with a bone." Think of each drip as an investment. I often use the analogy of building a house. Working from a good blueprint, you begin by building a solid foundation, a process which can be, dirty, difficult and not very rewarding. But it's an essential step that must be done before you can start putting up walls. Unfortunately, too many advisors start building foundations, but if the results don't come quickly enough, they fold up their tents and start building again elsewhere.

How long should one drip before calling it quits? That is not the issue. The issue is who you are dripping on. You could be throwing good money after bad, not because of the wrong technique but because of the wrong prospects. That said, it's a good idea to probe the prospect subtly from time to time. For example, you might say, "I fully understand that you're going to want to take your time before making a decision of this importance. If I can be so bold, am I on the right track? Are you getting good value from what I'm sending you, and do I have your permission to continue? Or should I call it a day?"

Who knows how long it might take for a prospect to warm up to you? However, if you had to decide whether to send out one letter to five hundred suspects/prospects or to send a series of five letters to one hundred good prospects, you know which approach I'm going to endorse.

I have known advisors who have dripped on prospects as many as forty-eight times before they came onside. Interestingly, those prospects – the ones who really make you work for it – often go on to be among your best clients. You know you're on track when they refer people to you before they themselves come on side.

In short, target your prospects well and follow the advice offered by some of the most grizzled advisors in the business: "Drip on them until they buy or die."

Let's look at other prospecting vehicles available to you.

The Telephone

As I mentioned earlier, the phone is a powerful tool, but should be used as a complement to your prospecting letters. That said, if you are currently cold calling and realizing a meaningful level of success, don't eliminate it immediately. Use it to hedge the slow transition to implementing your first string of three-letter drips. I've known several advisors who reduced their cold calling by fifty to seventy percent while using 3-step letter campaigns to target other prospects. The advisors found their performance on the phone increased immensely when they were no longer solely reliant on it to generate business.

The following introduction is offered as a simple yet effective cold calling technique to a prospect:

- "Good afternoon, (first name). I'm sorry to bother you; I know you're busy, so I'll be very brief. My name is John Dough, and I was wondering if I could take just two minutes to introduce myself and get your permission to forward some information that explains everything I do for my clients, many of whom are (geographic or demographic prospect commonality)?"

It's important, when connecting with someone for the first time, to radiate constrained enthusiasm in a respectful tone of voice. The phraseology you choose is essential to being persuasive. Here are several of my more favoured approaches:

- "I know your time is valuable, and I don't take that lightly. I want you to hold me accountable that this conversation will be a good use of your time."

Based on your prospect's response and once you get some momentum going, ask questions that will open the person up:

- "What do you expect from a financial advisor?"

or

- "What traits do you look for in a financial advisor?"

Probe further and ask the prospect to take action:

- "I don't want to claim miracles. Whenever I meet with someone to evaluate their financial plan, one of two things will happen. I either validate for them that their current plan is sound and that they shouldn't change a thing, or I reveal a few flaws that need adjusting. As you know, minor adjustments can often lead to major improvements. Either way, I can assure you that my 45-minute personalized needs analysis meeting will be a good use of your time."

Entire books are dedicated to the subject of telephone sales, so I don't pretend that these brief examples are everything you need to know. However, I encourage you to apply the same fundamentals that you would in other prospecting efforts. Be very focused on whom you call. Again, my favourite prospects tend to be business owners, many of whom have a soft spot for someone with a good phone attitude and acumen. It's better to call either early in the day or late in the afternoon or early evening. At those times, they tend to be the only ones in the office. Also, always prepare a script and stick with it. You can't wing it. Even if it's a point-form guideline, use something.

When you get rejected, always leave the call on a positive note:

- "I completely understand that now is not a good time. I appreciate your time and would like to ask you one final thing if I could. Do I have permission to touch base with you occasionally and forward timely information that I feel would be relevant to your situation?"

Either a yes or a no is a good response. You have the prospect's permission to continue or you can call it a day.

Trade Shows

As with all prospecting, a good trade show must be well-targeted. It makes sense to set up a booth at an event that will be attended by clients and prospects within a demographic or geographic sector. This far into the book, you know I'm going to stipulate that you not just show up. Consider a ramp-up campaign which includes inviting people to drop by and meet you at your booth. Consider the sizzle factor too. Perhaps a golf net or fly fishing simulator would be a good addition. Be certain that you have a good sifting mechanism and a strong call-to-action. The following is a classic textbook technique that one advisor used successfully:

The advisor created a number of simple Investment Tool Kits, which consisted of an abridged version of Peter Lynch's *Learn to Earn* audiocassette, several reports and a few reprinted articles. The advisor greeted people at the booth. When he connected well with someone, he would probe that person with a non-threatening statement: "You know, it's amazing how many people I've spoken with today who are a little confused about all the different options and decisions they have to consider." The advisor was fishing for an affirmative "Me too" response. If the prospect embraced the question, the advisor would continue: "I've got to tell you that the thing I like most about what I do is helping people make informed decisions about their financial futures. As you know, financial success is a matter or choice, not chance. To correct that old cliché, what you don't know CAN hurt you. I say that because everyone's financial situation is unique. Everyone has different needs. I'm not sure where I caught you with respect to your financial progress, but I'd like to offer something to you. [Pulls out the coupon for a kit]. I created this unique investment kit to help people make better choices about their investments. I had a bunch of them made so they didn't cost me much. If you think it might be of help, take this coupon and drop by my office, fax it, mail it or just give me a call on Monday and I'll get one out to you."

The advisor pointed to the bottom of the coupon where it suggested that quantities were limited. He then asked for the person's business card so that he could start receiving the advisor's newsletter. Once the prospect left the booth, the advisor wrote down observations he had made about the person on the back of the card. During the run of the trade show, the advisor met with and handed out over one hundred and fifty of his coupons. He collected ninety business cards. A week after the show had ended, fifteen people had called him for the kit, ten of whom were people who gave him their cards. When he sent the kits, he included a bonus report and an offer for a personalized needs analysis. The advisor sent his newsletter out to those who didn't order the kit and reminded them of it. Another six responses were received. The advisor ended up with five new clients within a month of the trade show. The rest of the people have become predisposed prospects that he continues to drip on.

As I mentioned earlier, the approach he used is called *risk-reversal*, also known as the 'puppy dog close.' The prospects incurred no risk in ordering the kit. The advisor took the risk that someone ordering the kit would use the information and not reciprocate. The bonus report and the offer for a personalized needs analysis are features called *bounce backs*. These particular bounce backs were designed to induce the recipient to call again after they had received what they had ordered.

It's not uncommon for a retail company to enclose a special limited time offer for further purchases when they ship an order. This offer capitalizes on a customer's enthusiasm for the highly-anticipated product they are receiving. For example, Quicken software would include a five-dollar rebate to recipients of the free diskette should they order the software package within a limited period of time.

An advisor client of ours, who was promoting an oil and gas limited partnership, asked prospects to order an informative videocassette that outlined the opportunity. For people who ordered, we suggested the advisor include a package of microwave popcorn – to ensure the prospect actually watched the video – and an invitation to a dinner seminar. The unexpected invitation included an menu card which asked the prospect to select either a chicken dish or a pasta dinner and to fax back the card. Response to the bounce back was good, and so too was the attendance and subsequent conversion. (The pasta was so-so.)

Everything I just described is considered textbook prospecting. Both advisors offered value, relied on the contrast principle, positioned themselves as Number Two, created urgency and acquired leads or predisposed prospects. And all of it was accomplished while taking the high road.

Print Advertising

As you have probably already gathered, I seldom recommend print advertising. Most ads are glorified business cards and can't be counted on to do anything but stroke an advisor's ego or build a little name recognition. It's time to look at the exceptions, and for that reason I'll give you couple of ideas.

At the risk of sounding painfully repetitive, be targeted. Ensure that your ads are placed in publications that are read by a high concentration of your clients and target-market pillars. I would rather you run an ad in a trade magazine for dentists than in a city-wide newspaper. Remember, you are trying to build an insider's reputation within your target markets, so be certain that your ads radiate that by way of phraseology, etc.

As you do with the letters you send out, be certain that the top of your ad uses a headline that conveys a compelling benefit or presents a problem. Your company name and logo is not a benefit, so keep it to the bottom in a small and understated manner.

Make your ad compelling, not a boring smattering of words. Some advisors have had better success showing a picture taken at a seminar of themselves with a guest speaker. Others have used a Q & A format, which imparts an advertorial feel. Others have simply run an ad, showing the advisor handing a cheque to a charitable organization or to the winner of a high school mutual fund selection contest.

In the call-to-action, make it easy for prospects to call you. Offer something tangible in the form of a special report, kit or audio-cassette. Some advisors have created a voice mail information centre and used it as part of their calls-to-action. The ad directs prospects to call a 24-hour information line on which the advisor passes along timely and topical investment strategies. At the end of the four or five minute message, the advisor invites investors with a minimum portfolio of one hundred thousand dollars to call him directly to receive an information kit and personalized needs analysis. As many as twenty-five suspects might call because the information centre is valuable but non-threatening. Perhaps five of those will actually leave their names and addresses. It's another example of great sifting and lead acquisition using an inexpensive and hands-off technique.

Whatever you do, avoid running staid "here-I-am" ads. Most ads by advisors are glorified business cards. They sometimes will include a picture of the advisor – perhaps on the phone, trying to look busy. (Maybe the photographer was too pressed for time and couldn't wait for the advisor to get off the phone!) Then the ad has a headline and vanilla feature dump and then the call-to-action that usually says something like this: "Call me to receive a complementary review of your portfolio."

Just out of curiosity, when was the last time you received this call from a prospect: "Hi. You don't know me but you seem like a nice person. I was wondering if you would conduct a complimentary review of my portfolio for me." Approximately? Never! And don't try to rationalize an ad like the one I described because of the fact that you'll get good "name recognition." A good ad with a good call-to-action will get you just as much name recognition. The difference is, your phone will ring!

With respect to advertising in the yellow pages, be certain that your point of difference is in your call-to-action. Examine what your competitors are asking prospects to do, and then ensure that you are perceived as more professional and helpful. It's more labour-intensive, but it's well worth the effort. Incidentally, never tell people to "See our ad in the Yellow Pages" in any of your other marketing vehicles. You are essentially giving all of your competitors free exposure. Make reference to your listing in the "White Pages" where your name isn't surrounded by other advisors.

Also, in keeping with spaced repetition, run a series if you are going to commit to print advertising. Seldom will one ad alone make your phone or fax machine light up.

Seminars

Seminars rank among the top marketing strategies available, so much so that the ability to present a seminar is explained in greater detail in the next section. For the time being, let me reiterate the basics. As always, be focused and be targeted. Again, the question is not how many people attend your events, but who attends. Consider client dinners and/or presenting small in-house lunch-and-learn seminars to companies within a target market. I know advisors who have successfully run events at engineering firms, high tech firms; they've even gone into dental offices after hours for the benefit of the hygienists.

Consider a series of three sessions over a three-week period rather than one long event. Three twenty-minute sessions on three consecutive Thursdays is far more productive than a one-hour event. It's not uncommon for fifteen people to show up at the first event, many of whom simply want to eat the sandwiches and juice you brought. At the second event, don't be disappointed if only nine show up and only five at the third event. The likelihood of you closing those five after sifting them from the other ten suspects is quite good.

Always provide a handout so that each attendee can take notes. Include a take-away item such as a book, pen, mug or mouse pad.

Have a prize draw that ties in with your question-and-answer period, and use a variation of the "either/or" needs analysis close as described in the trade show example. You can introduce the certificate by combining it with an evaluation form and asking for participant feedback.

For larger events, always have a VIP session beforehand for your best clients. Don't be surprised if it generates more business than the main event. Feature wine and cheese and have the speaker give an informal fireside chat for your top clients and their guests.

Be Selective

There are countless other prospecting vehicles available to you. There's everything from inexpensive geographic mail drops in affluent areas where you have clients to expensive billboard signs on major streets and highways. The options are limitless. Your job is to select the most efficient and effective one for your situation. Regarding efficiency, an important caveat is to be certain that you first test an approach and measure its performance before you engage in any significant campaign.

I could fill a book with stories of financial advisors who bought into marketing campaigns that were either inappropriate to their situation or flawed in some way.

One advisor I met up with was a marketing junkie. When someone tried to sell him an idea, his response was, "How many colours does it come in?" He bought a prospecting seminar-in-a-box that ate up incredible amounts of time and money but which only attracted mediocre prospects. (Talk about mistaking movement for achievement.) He bought an esoteric software program that enabled him to blanket the marketplace with letters that made him out to be a huckster. He bought a thousand audiocassette business cards and mailed them to prospects. Meanwhile, he had over five hundred *clients* on whom he rarely spent a dime, and he would wonder why he kept losing them and why he was generating so few referrals. He was sold on concepts that were glitzy and made for great stories, but they were ultimately inappropriate.

Another advisor, approached by an advertising company, was sold an extensive yet completely flawed direct mail campaign and newspaper advertising package. When he rolled the mail campaign out, it bombed. When I asked the advisor what the advertising company knew about the financial services industry, he said, "Come to think about it, they never once mentioned that they had a client in my field. All they gushed about were their awards for creativity and design."

I remember telling him that, had he been selling breakfast cereal or stereos, creativity might have come in handy. When you are marketing financial services and the promise of the future, you can't hire someone who hasn't been around the block. Only use marketing strategies that can be measured and quantified. Campaigns that have you haphazardly inundating the marketplace with reckless abandon might stir up some activity, but you can't operate spasmodically. You need predictability.

The Law of Expectation says that what you can conceive, believe and expect will often be achieved. Focus single-mindedly on your marketing activities, and the productivity will take care of itself. Therefore, scrutinize your marketing initiatives to see what they can bring you.

The Numbers Tell The Whole Story

Athletes focus on their statistics. Big businesses focus on their systems. An airline knows that it costs 8.3 cents to fly a seat on a airplane one mile. After factoring in the wages, lease of the aircraft, fuel, advertising, terminal fees and insurance, they are able to determine how cheaply they can sell a ticket while still making a profit.

A company which sells high-quality personalized pens runs ads in four major financial publications. After describing its unique product offering, they invite interested prospects to call to receive a free catalog. In each publication, readers are directed to ask for a specific extension number, each of which is different. For example, if the ad ran in *Worth* magazine, the extension might be WM1. If the ad ran in *Forbes* magazine, the extension could be FM1, and so on. Based on the frequency of requests, the company can decide which ads to continue to run and which ones to pull. Without this type of quantification tool, they would have no idea which magazine is performing well for them and which is not.

Virtually every marketing activity you engage in can be quantified in some way too.

For example, take the financial advisor who hired two cold callers. After an unsuccessful attempt on my part to have him consider other options (he kept bragging about a couple of big clients – excuse me, customers – that he had landed because of the callers), I asked him point blank, "Tell me the numbers," meaning, *Tell me how many calls have to be made to land confirmed sales.* He had no idea. All he knew was that occasionally, his callers had stumbled onto some business. After asking him several more questions, I very quickly uncovered this simple formula:

If one of his cold callers dialed the phone one hundred times, that person would connect with about thirty-five suspects. (The other sixty-five people couldn't be reached, the receptionist got in the way, voice mail clicked in or the answerer simply hung up.) Of the thirty-five suspects, six warmed to the pitch and agreed to the offer of a free portfolio review. Of those six prospects, one became a customer or client. So, what we now know is that every time the cold caller dials the phone one hundred times, the advisor will get a new client. The advisor no longer bogs the caller down with abstract productivity goals beyond his or her control. He or she simply dials the phone and pitches those who will listen. The trickle-down effect takes over from there. Furthermore, if the caller leaves the advisor, he simply hands the system to the new caller. Interestingly, when it comes to a new cold caller, the numbers don't change. Only the face does.

The bottom line is that every marketing approach must be able to justify and pay for itself. There are exceptions. If you were to rent a billboard near a highway off-ramp that fed into a retirement lifestyle community you were targeting, it would be hard to measure its impact. But try anyway. In keeping with the "inspect what you expect" adage, survey people for feedback and based on the comments you receive, decide if it's worthwhile. Ultimately, business is a numbers game.

One advisor did just that. She asked a great client if he had seen her firm's billboard sign and if so, what he had thought of it. The client mentioned that he had seen it but had found it too crammed with information in order to be read. He was bang on. A billboard is seen in a blink of an eye. It can only sell one idea and must convey a clear benefit or present an important problem that needs solving. The advisor changed her board and sure enough, instantly received positive feedback from other clients and prospects, including the client who had made the suggestion.

Incidentally, another advisor received a suggestion from a client that he add mini infomercials that people could listen to when their phone calls were placed on hold. Towards that end, the advisor created a "Did you know?" campaign and uncovered some client assets and disability insurance business because of it. What is great is that the ads are informative rather than just trying to sell something, and his clients appreciate that distinction.

Speaking of numbers, I'm reminded of a situation that should describe this point well. By now, you must have determined that I love to golf. I'm not a great player but when I do, I always try to be the one who keeps score. When a friend I'm playing with has a bad hole, I'll tend to rub it in a little. We'll move on to the next tee box and I'll say, "What did you get on the last hole?" even though I know his score full well. Invariably, he'll start to rattle off a long-winded story. I'll interrupt him: "Look, it's a small box. It's too small for a story. It will only hold a number. But the number will tell the whole story. So what's the number?"

When it comes to marketing, it's a small box as well. Know your numbers.

Test

Being able to quantify your marketing efforts enables you to avoid what Paul McCartney refers to as 'anticipointment.' An important step in that avoidance is, before you commit to any significant campaign, test it first. Before you send out letters to five hundred prospects, send out fifty first and measure the response. If it's poor, it probably won't get any better if you send out the other four hundred and fifty. Take a microscope to every marketing effort and relentlessly scrutinize its capabilities.

If the response to a test is reasonable, make a few minor adjustments to perfect it even further. Remember, minor adjustments really can lead to major improvements. Something as simple as using a yellow highlighter on a key point or adding a post-it note with a hand-written message can lead to an improvement in response. W. Edwards Deming, the genius who helped revitalize the Japanese economy after the Second World War, discovered that every process could be refined and improved. He called this practice of fine-tuning The Law of Optimization. The Japanese word for it is *kaizen*, which means 'constant improvement.' Sam Walton of Wal-Mart fame referred to it as 'constant tinkering.' Once you test a campaign and can quantify its performance, you'll be more likely to experience measurable progress in a more reasonable period of time.

New Adventures in Prospecting

To paraphrase Thomas Edison, if there is a better way to do some-thing, find it. All marketing should be well-conceived. Most errors in judgment are made when you are in a hurry. Never leave the writing of a letter that will be sent out tomorrow until the day before. Write it and put it away for a few days. You will be far more objective. Give it to someone in your network to critique.

Reflecting back to the Law of Attraction, I'd like to close this section on prospecting by having you ask yourself these questions: "What strategies do I need to employ? What kind of person do I need to become in order to attract the very best prospects?" We're ready for the next section of the book.

Chapter 4

The Qualities of an Effective Advisor

The Qualities of an Effective Advisor

E ver since I began working with financial advisors, I have been
determined to find out what separates the best from the rest.
Why is it that in the same marketplace, some financial advisors are
dramatically more successful than others are? The metaphor that
keeps coming to mind is that, while the winds of opportunity blow
the same for everybody, some people arrive at their destinations
while others drift off course. Clearly, every ambitious advisor starts
out with good intentions but in time, the gulf between the best and
the rest widens.

A host of qualities contribute to an effective advisor. Some relate to
acumen while others are attitudinal. This section is dedicated to
those qualities that I consider the most essential from a marketing
perspective. In my opinion, when it comes to success in this business,
you're a marketer first and financial advisor second. Don't misinter-
pret that statement. It is essential that you have a high level of financial awareness. However, marketing – the ability to attract and keep
good clients – is more often than not the key to helping advisors
achieve their goals.

Quality #1: Designing the Future
Far and away, the most important quality among the "captains of
commerce" is the ability to design and stick with a plan. A marketing

plan is an essential tool, serving as a guidance system as the year unfolds. Like an architect who follows a blueprint, a financial advisor has to make time to plan the year out on paper and to crystallize his or her goals, including the activities that will lead there.

Consider this analogy: If you ever go to the Kennedy Space Center in Cape Canaveral, you will discover that the space shuttle lifts off at such speed that its computers are continually making midcourse corrections because of the vehicle's tendency to drift. We drift too. A marketing plan serves as our computer correction system, helping to bring us back on track. As you know, our direction today determines our destination tomorrow. The course we've set for ourselves helps us to stay focused on reaching our destination.

Put another way, if you were to look down a highway, you might notice a slight camber, or arc, on the surface, which is designed to ensure that the rain drains away. If I were to drive down the highway and take my hands off the wheel, in short order that bow on the road's surface would cause my car to veer towards the ditch (which would annoy my wife to no end). As Jim Morrison often sang, "Keep your eyes on the road, and your hands up on the wheel."

It's the same with your future. You need a plan. It's not a question of whether or not you'll arrive but where, and do you have a plan to take you there?

Achieve on Purpose

Every advisor I've met faces the future with either anticipation or apprehension. Those who face it with apprehension do so because their future is not well designed. These people operate on a moment-by-moment basis, perpetually overwhelmed because their day consists of putting out fires and dealing with sporadic activities. This type of approach can ensure a certain measure of success, but it is a mundane existence. At the end of the day, you ultimately feel powerless without a plan and at the mercy of events beyond your control.

When my company works one-to-one with an advisor, we ask that person to think about the long-term costs associated with short-term thinking. We want our client to take the long-term view, *looking forward* to the future with a robust attitude.

What I'm ultimately saying is that you just can't ignore the impact of operating with a plan. It becomes your promise of the future. Armed with that promise, you will be more inclined to pay the price, to sacrifice small amounts of instant satisfaction for the huge rewards that stem from delayed gratification.

It reminds me of the story of an airline pilot who flew small commercial jets for a regional airline. He decided to step down to a first officer's position in order to fly larger jets for a bigger airline. It meant a drop in pay, but that was his dream. He could have stayed where he was, but his real goal – the one that represented true meaning and purpose – would have eluded him.

As an entrepreneur, you owe it to yourself to build your own dream. According to sales and marketing expert Brian Tracy, "Those without goals or a plan are always destined to work for those who have them." And as Oliver Wendell Holmes once stated, "There are three kinds of people: those who make things happen, those who watch what happens, and those who say, "What happened?"

At this point, I'm sure I've made it painfully clear about the importance of having a plan. Let's now look at the process of designing one. Let me first say that I am not a big fan of a tedious longwinded fifteen-page report that you will never look at again. The process of writing such a plan is a good exercise, but it's a difficult reference tool to use as the year unfolds. (The longest plan I have ever developed for an advisor has been about four pages in length.)

Observations

I begin the creation of the plan with a section called **Observations**, where I outline what I consider to be the advisor's unique selling proposition, that person's prospective target markets, areas that need special attention and those in which the advisor seems especially vulnerable.

During this process, I discuss various scenarios with the advisor. (Many of the world's best business planners use this technique with their clients.) As you know, events can take place in this business that are beyond your control but which can still have a significant impact on what you do. For example, you have to consider *critical volatilities*. These are events that can catch you by surprise, such as marketing seminars that normally produce good results but start dwindling, or a reliable promotional partner who retires. You also have to consider reliable certainties, events that are, for the most part, predictable and within your control, such as referrals from clients or a steadily improving demographic target market. Finally, you must anticipate your worst nightmares. For some people, it might mean that their firm is merging with a competitor who has a radically different and conflicting philosophy than theirs. For others, it could be a stock market meltdown. I often remind advisors of the positive power that comes with negative thinking. I ask them if they have 'bullet-proofed' their clients and tempered their clients' expectations. What are their clients' perceptions of the advisor? Are they positive?

Desired Results

After the Observations section, I outline the advisor's goals and objectives in a section titled **Desired Results**. Goals are powerful motivators that serve as your vision and promise of the future, adding to one's confidence and optimism. Interestingly, the Japanese word for *optimism* means "having enough challenges to give life meaning and purpose." As I mentioned earlier, people without goals feel powerless and at the mercy of events beyond their control. Goal setters, on the other hand, "boldly go" with the sense of purpose to look beyond short-term obstacles. It's no different than a value investor looking beyond one year's modest results on an investment they plan to hold for a long time. They know that in the end, their patience will pay off, unlike those investors who keep chasing last year's achievers.

When I sit down with advisors to discuss their goals, I ask them three questions. First, where do they see themselves in twelve months? Secondly, why is that destination important to them? And finally, what kind of person do they need to become to make that picture a reality?

Activities

As I often mention, my job is to help an advisor sift through all of the marketing activities available in order to select those that are most relevant to his or her situation. The **Activities** section reminds us of the importance of the Law of Cause and Effect, which states that our activities determine our productivity and that in order to increase our productivity, we have to select the activities that will give us the highest yield.

Before you start a journey, you always study the destination. As Stephen Covey suggests, you have to begin with the end in mind. It's no different in business planning. If one's direction does in fact determine one's destination, you have to be certain not to select activities that are flawed or incompatible with your personal style.

I've seen too many advisors get sold on a multitude of marketing ideas without giving a thought to whether or not the idea was appropriate, what the activities involved would be about, or where the ideas would ultimately take them. They simply hoped to duplicate what are often inflated claims.

The Activities section is like writing a screenplay. Whether you're an established or novice advisor, the clarity that comes from the Activities section is necessary in defining the activities that will lead to your productivity goals.

Ongoing and Focused Marketing Campaigns

There are two types of marketing activities, *ongoing* and *focused* campaigns. Ongoing activities would be classified as things you do throughout the year in response to relevant circumstances. For example, the New Client Welcome process is something you would roll out every time a new client came on board. Call rotations, referral recognition and client delights also fit in this category.

For prospects that you are committed to dripping on until they come on side, this too would be classified as an ongoing activity. This means that every month, they are receiving something from you. The key here is to spread the initiative out throughout the month. If you have two hundred prospects, program your contact management system to send out ten letters a day. In case you are wondering (and this applies to both clients and prospects), you can't send out too much information. "How much?" is not the question. It's "how dull" that is the real issue. If your drips are informative and they have some pizzazz, prospects and clients alike will look forward to receiving them.

Focused campaigns are activities that lead up to a deadline, such as preparations for a seminar, client dinner or trade show. Those campaigns would typically have a four to eight week ramp-up window during which three-step letter campaigns and phone follow-ups take place. Other focused campaigns would include target marketing to a group you have selected, such as offering estate planning or wealth management kits to business owners.

Since most marketing plans contain anywhere from six to twelve focused campaigns varying between one or two months in length, your focused campaigns can either stand alone or be thematically linked.

Wrapping It Up
The end of the plan is simply titled **In Conclusion**. This section reminds the advisor to stay the course. Too many people (myself included) from all walks of business life suffer from the 'light at the end of the tunnel syndrome.' It seems that as people execute their plans and gather momentum, they start to taste success and thus try to speed things up. Next thing you know, they are deviating from what they had laid out, trying out new ideas rather than seeing their existing plans – the ones that worked so well – through to the end.

Stay faithful to proven disciplines in the early stages, even if the results are small. Don't get distracted by or get sold on a new idea while you've got a plan in process. Have tunnel vision. Most people fail during times of growth, not decline. In these situations, your decisions go a long way toward sculpting your character and determining your pace.

For example, I know advisors who have achieved great results from a simple plan consisting of FORM-related call rotations, welcome kits, milestones and client dinners, as well as a daily marketing "fourmula" that is composed of four client drips, four prospect drips and forty-four minutes of personal development, day-in, day-out.

Quality #2: Time Management

Right up front, I'm going to suggest that 'time management' is among the biggest misnomers in business. You can't manage time. The clock relentlessly charges forward, and there is nothing any of us can do about it. So why call it time management? Probably because most business people feel there isn't enough time in the day, and they wish they could add a few more hours to each one.

What's really interesting is that time is one of the only things that everyone has the same amount of. The most successful advisor and the struggling also-ran both have twenty-four hours in the day. The difference is in how they invest it.

Let me correct the old cliché that says, "Time is money." It isn't true. Time is more valuable than money. Think about it. When you invest your money in a marketing idea, it isn't a big deal if the idea doesn't work. You can go out and make more money. Not so with time. When it's spent, it's gone.

You probably do not make a practice of squandering money. Before you invest any, you always ask yourself, what will be my Return on Investment (or ROI)? I'm asking you to be that diligent with your time. Before you invest any, ask yourself, what is my Return on Energy? In other words, what is the best use of my time? The challenge is to determine which activities give you the highest return and focus single-mindedly on them.

As it relates to the Law of Cause and Effect, most effective advisors I've met are good at these five things:

They never major in minor things. They only do the things they really get paid to do. As you are probably aware, I'm convinced that you get paid to do three things: invest time with your clients, invest time with good prospects (not suspects), and invest time sharpening and refining your skills. With very few exceptions, every other activity is a means to an end, not an end in itself. Perhaps an assistant should be the one who executes them. What's intriguing to me is that an advisor making $80,000 a year seems just as busy as an advisor making $800,000. The problem is, the first advisor is more than likely mistaking movement for achievement.

I'm reminded of a seminar that I conducted some years ago for professional speakers. Having worked with presenters such as Jim Rohn and Brian Tracy, I learned quite a bit about the business, and in my seminar I shared this information with aspiring speakers. I challenged everyone in my audience to make a goal of writing a book. I suggested that by doing so, it would help them crystallize their thoughts by putting them on paper as well as serve to credentialize them as authorities in their fields (not to mention create an added income stream).

One woman in the audience raised her hand and told me that while she has always wanted to write a book, she simply couldn't find the time. I responded, "Isn't that interesting. Just today, on my flight in, I finished reading the book *The Road Ahead* by Bill Gates. And something tells me he's just a little bit busier than you are. Still, he found the time to write it."

As you have probably gathered, having a good marketing plan can help you squeeze more time out of the day by helping you become focused. Some people say that if they had more time, they'd make a plan. We both know that if they had a plan, they'd have more time.

They have a sense of urgency. Have you ever noticed how productive you are during the week leading up to a vacation? Deadlines have a habit of doing that. It's easier said than done, but the best don't procrastinate. They have a do-it-now attitude toward everything they do. I've come to realize that, while it's easier to put off a task that seems ominous, no task is as tough as your imagination leads you to believe it is. And the satisfaction that comes from accomplishing something before a deadline is pretty nice too.

They Block Time. The best are unreasonable with themselves and with their time, laying out the coming week in advance and blocking off time slots. Every activity they schedule falls within the '3C' daily guideline:

Compression: Days on which to concentrate all high-level, high-energy, high-ROE activities. These activities are the critical moments that should make the biggest impact on your life and your income.

Contribution: Days during which you focus on the activities that contribute to your compression days. These activities are a little harder to quantify, but are just as essential.

For example, during a four-hour game of golf, a professional golfer might actually spend only ninety seconds hitting the ball. Those ninety seconds are his critical moments. However, the rest of that four-hour game comprises his contribution time; what transpires during his contribution time has a significant impact on those moments when he is hitting the ball.

Cultivation: Days reserved for rewarding yourself and shoring up energy for compression and contribution days. As Zig Ziglar has often said, "Don't mistake activity for accomplishment." You might be working hard, but are you being productive? You have to decompress.

In a perfect world, each week should have two compression days, two contribution days and perhaps as many as three cultivation days. Some advisors follow this model and still manage to get more done in four days than others do in five or six. Critics might snicker at this model, implying that it's impractical. They are the same people who slave away fifty hours a week but only actually get thirty-five hours worth of work done.

I remember telling one of my clients never to read the paper or to eat at his office. My contention was that his office was not a retreat but a place to generate revenue. He would be better off reading the paper on his boat and having lunch with his wife or with clients, being at the office only when he had to be. Today, that advisor can't wait to get to work. He truly believes he is more productive now, even though he spends less time there.

When you create your own time schedule, discipline yourself not to deviate from it. You would never trivialize the importance of a client appointment. Then never trivialize the importance of your own time either. Be unreasonable with it. I'm not suggesting you become a robot – I'm well aware of the caged feeling that comes with scheduling that's too tight – but at the same time, don't think you're slacking off if you're not in the office.

They are incredibly efficient. You can do certain things in order to become more efficient. A four-hour seminar on speed-reading helped me considerably. Multi-task by doing two things at the same time without one interfering with the other. For example, listen to tapes in your car or on a Walkman while on a treadmill. I know a number of advisors who subscribe to *Executive Summaries,* the monthly package of business book summaries that I described earlier. Others will clip articles for quick review rather than leafing through the entire magazine again.

They don't try to do it all. For some advisors, the biggest business breakthrough they ever realized came when they started outsourcing low ROE activities to services such as professional newsletter producers and database managers or when they hired a marketing assistant who did the lesser ROE activities. The bottom line is this: if an advisor wants to make $300 an hour, he or she had better not be doing $30-an-hour activities. However, there are precautions you must take, which serves as a nice segue to our next quality.

Quality #3: Leadership – The Driving Force

As I mentioned, bringing on someone to do the lower return activities in order to free you up to do what you do best might be just the ticket. I think it's worth mentioning again that you are paid to do three things: talk to clients and partners, talk to good prospects and refine your skills. Everything else is secondary, and the more of those activities you can hand over, the more time you will have to do business. For some advisors, their assistants have gone on to become associate advisors responsible for working with the eighty-percent clients, freeing the advisor to work more closely with the all important twenty-percent. But it hasn't been a perfect situation for all who have done so.

It's true that a marketing assistant can often be more beneficial than any other marketing instrument, but you have to remember that you now have someone who is dependent upon you for guidance and direction. Which explains why leadership is such an essential quality of success.

There are three important skills needed in being a leader: selecting good people, leading good people and knowing when and how to disassociate from not-so-good people.

Selection is Everything!

Half the battle in being a good leader is in hiring people who want to be led. There are a lot of ambitious, eager people out there, so select the best you can. Be on the lookout for clues that a candidate might not be compatible with you. Overlooking obvious flaws can be costly.

I have always found my best people through people I already know. Ask a friend, co-worker or business associate if he or she might know of someone to fit the role. It works just as the Law of 52 does with your clients – the people you know might know someone who would be a perfect fit. (If not, run an ad, contact an employment service or contact your firm's human resources department.)

When meeting with a prospective assistant for the first time, it's important to uncover that person's aptitude and attitude. Both are critical. Keep in mind, however, that aptitude is easier to teach and develop than attitude.

Start the meeting off on the right foot by putting the applicant in a relaxed and open frame of mind. Start by saying, "Right up front, let's be relaxed and comfortable during our meeting. Remember you're interviewing me as well, so let's make this as painless as possible."

Be certain not to try to sell the person on the job even if your intuition is telling you that this person is The One. Also, don't rule out anyone unless that person is downright incompatible. Remember that you aren't trying to hire someone like yourself. You're hiring someone who will complement your skills and offset some of your shortcomings.

During interviews, look for clues regarding the candidates' willingness or reluctance to work hard. They might be well qualified, suggesting that they *can* do certain tasks, but what's more important is *will* they do them?

Here are a few tips for conducting a good interview:

- Ask questions that make the person reflect on his or her past. Ask, "What are your proudest achievements?"

- Ask questions that cause the person to look into the future. Ask, "Where do you see yourself in five years?"

- Ask questions about the candidate's commitment to self-development. "What do you consider to be your greatest strength or asset?" "What do you consider to be your weakness?" "What do you do to sharpen your skills?"

You are trying to reveal the person's core beliefs and motivators. If you are going to work closely with this person, ask yourself, "Do I like this person enough to want them to baby-sit my kids or have them over for a Sunday barbecue?"

It's a good indication if, rather than bragging, the candidate responds to your questions with intelligent questions of his or her own, not just the transparent questions about pay and working hours but those about upside potential and so on.

Create a short list of candidates. If you feel you've got a winner, arrange for a second meeting a few days later. In the meantime, give the applicant a book to read or a couple of business-related cassettes to listen to so that he or she can provide you with a synopsis during the second meeting. Always interview someone at least twice and, if possible, have a second person conduct an interview for you. (I always ask a woman to sit in on one of the meetings because of her considerable practicality and intuition.)

Always investigate references. Ask previous employers if, given the opportunity, they would hire this person again. You can't always gauge responses. No matter how thinly you slice it, there are always two sides to a story. The candidate might have left a previous employment for reasons unrelated to ability. However, past success generally is indicative of future success.

Once you've selected a prospective assistant, implement a 90-day probationary period during which you evaluate that person's progress. I was taught that before I get into anything, I better know how to get out. It's expensive to hire someone, but not nearly as expensive as it can be to fire someone. Understand the law and your rights and responsibilities.

You may find yourself having to make a change following the probationary period. If the person objects to the 90-day review, don't bring them onside. People are like opportunities; another one will always come along.

Income should be a base salary plus an incentive program based on the person's contributions to your bottom line.

When you bring someone onside, lay out your expectations clearly, establish quantifiable goals and then bury them in work. Don't find yourself in a situation where the new recruit is standing at your office doorway, asking what to do next. Get out of the way and challenge that person intensively.

Establish a weekly meeting time, and don't waver from it. This meeting has to be viewed with the same level of importance that you give to one with a client or prospect. The more importance you place on it, the more seriously your assistant will view it. Make the meeting predictable and have the marketing assistant direct it. Not only should your assistant look forward to the meeting, but he or she has to bring value to it via progress reports, research and observations. If not, the meeting will be nothing more than a forum where you can hear yourself speak.

All of your actions throughout the day have an impact on your assistant. Nothing goes unnoticed. Leadership is the ability to bring out in people what they might not bring forward on their own.

Here is a simple leadership self-analysis:

- Do you exude a sense of speed and urgency?
- Are you calm in times of uncertainty?

- Are you resilient, almost awe-inspiring in crises?
- Are you unusually kind to people, be they service people in restaurants, cab drivers or people along your lines of contacts: the very people who connect with your clients?
- Do you eliminate fear and intimidation in the work environment?
- Do you take responsibility when there is a breakdown, and pass the praise when there is a breakthrough?
- Do you disguise orders for suggestions?
- Do you empower people by giving them challenges?
- Do you correct mistakes rather than criticize people?

Remember, you have a tremendous responsibility – whether you want it or not – of being a mentor. One of the greatest investments you'll ever make is in another person.

More than simply having an impact on a job, you are having an impact on your assistant's life and future. Ask yourself how you affect others. Do you leave a profit? Personally, I always sponsor kids for a skate-a-thon or give money when they are canvassing for a charity or selling chocolates to raise money for a school or community centre. And I do this not because I believe in the cause but because I want that kid to feel empowered and optimistic when he or she walks away from my house. Fifteen bucks for a few stale packages of chocolate is a great investment, for no other reason than the look on the child's face. You never know whom you're speaking with and how your contribution will affect that person's life. The point is this: if I would do that for a child I don't know, why wouldn't I apply the same philosophy for an associate who can make an impact upon my future?

Be Encouraging

When your assistant presents an idea, embrace it. The worst thing you can do is squash, suppress or make light of ideas and input. Lead by example when it comes to doing some of the less glamorous work. Show that you are not above licking and sticking stamps to help get out a letter campaign to prospects. It reminds me of something my wife said regarding exercise. Rather than telling me that I should work out more, she suggested that "we" should get more exercise. It was a small but powerful distinction.

In some of the work I've done with branch managers, I've taken a train-the-trainer approach to help these managers light a fire under their teams. I'm always reminded of the advice of Confucius, who said, "Give a man a fish and you feed him for a day. Teach a man to fish and you feed him for a lifetime."

That said, there will be times where you will ask yourself, is this person hurting me more than they're helping? Before you take action during this time of uncertainty, identify what really is the problem. You might not, for instance, be providing the right environment. It might come back to the issue of incompatibility. Don't overlook the fact that there could also be a temporary problem in that person's life. Give him or her the benefit of the doubt. Ask if something is bothering them, in several different ways if you have to, in order to uncover the issue.

If your assistant's attitude is good but his or her skills are lacking, it might be in your best interest to hang in there. As Confucius, in his infinite wisdom, said elsewhere, "When the student is ready, the teacher will appear." By and large, an assistant is as good as the encouragement and guidance they receive. Reason, however, must always triumph over sentiment. You can't want people to succeed more than they do.

Quality #4: The Art of Persuasion

Marketing is the ability to attract and get in front of good people. Selling is what takes place once you're in front of them. While mine is a marketing book, it is my personal fascination with selling that prompted me to include this section as one of the seven essential qualities.

What really amazes me is that if you asked the most successful advisors for their secrets to sales success, chances are they couldn't tell you. Selling is not an exact science nor is it a technical or analytical skill. I truly believe it is an art form, one that requires a thorough understanding of human nature and personalities.

Most sales training courses suggest that selling is a complex process.

Based on what top advisors have taught me, I'm more inclined to say that selling is less complicated than that. Without putting it too simply, the art of persuasion is about being likable and about having an ability to build confidence in the minds of your prospects.

As with many things, to raise your skill level in a certain area you sometimes first need to take a step back before taking two steps forward. (My golf score actually increased after a lesson, before it improved.) In selling, unless you're doing everything perfectly, making refinements can be uncomfortable at first, but improvements will soon follow.

Preparation is Paramount

Preparation is as important as actual selling technique because you can get a prospect into a predisposed frame of mind before he or she even walks through your door. Send your prospects a pre-meeting questionnaire or confirmation card. Some advisors go so far as to send an impressive kit or item determined by information they gathered from the prospect while making the appointment.

I'll give you an example of what I mean. An advisor received a phone call from the father of one of his preferred clients. The father mentioned that his son had recommended he call to arrange a meeting to discuss his current financial strategy. The topic of demographics came up in the conversation, and the advisor asked the man if he had read David Foot's book *Boom, Bust and Echo*. The father, who clearly was worth a lot of money, mentioned that he was interested in reading it, but he was twelfth on the waiting list at the library.

After a nice chat, the advisor booked the appointment for the following week and ended the call. He then took a copy of the book, of which he had several, and dropped it off at his client's – the father's eldest son – office with a post-it note on the book that read, "Could you give this to your dad to read? I thought I'd lend him my copy. Have him bring it in when he comes for our meeting."

The father was so impressed with the gesture. The advisor could have given one of his copies of the book to send him (heck, the father could have probably bought the company that published the book, he was *that* well off), but the advisor had noted that the man was a frugal person who would value the gesture of a loan more.

The meeting lasted about an hour. The advisor discussed his financial plan for a grand total of about ten minutes. The father dominated the conversation, reliving stories of his glory years and so on. The advisor had improved his own odds as well as met an extremely predisposed prospect.

Once the appointment is set, prepare by studying your prospect as thoroughly as you would any of your products. Study that person's company or industry – you can even go so far as to study the origin of the person's name using the Internet. Whatever gives you the chance to make intelligent references and observations during the conversation will help you immensely.

Let that obsession for preparation carry forward to the actual meeting itself. Most top advisors spend fifteen to thirty minutes just prior to the meeting preparing themselves.

Many will record their meetings to uncover ways to refine their skills, or they will create a one-page bullet-form list of key notes from the meeting for future review.

Never wing it or go into a meeting with an "I can't wait to hear what falls out of my mouth" approach. You should have your core presentation so nailed down that someone could call you at three in the morning, wake you up and say, "Give me the pitch." Change your audience, not your message. However, don't completely bottle your pitch with a "stop me if you hear something you like" or "insert name here" spiel.

Be Interested

The key to an effective one-to-one presentation is to be interested before trying to be interesting. A good meeting is essentially a conversation. For some advisors I've met, their biggest liability was their own personality, not because they weren't good people but because when they engaged in a conversation, they tried too hard to win the person over by feature dumping. Contrived, slick presentations don't radiate a confident advisor-of-choice feel.

The pendulum can swing in your favour if you've dedicated the early stages of the conversation to uncovering the prospect's hot buttons and gauging your presentation around them. If you dominate the conversation, the prospect may appear to be paying attention, but he or she could actually be bursting at the seams, wanting to get in at least two cents. As the prospect is listening to you, that person starts formulating unspoken objections that might never get addressed.

It reminds me of a story I read about Mark McCormack, founder of IMG, the world's largest sports agent and production firm, which represents Wayne Gretzky, Joe Montana and countless other stars (including me, he wishes). Mark wrote the book *What They Don't Teach You at Harvard Business School*, among other great books. He got his start by convincing Arnold Palmer, Jack Nicklaus and Gary Player to let him represent them. The story of how he got Palmer onside is quite interesting.

As a lawyer, Mark was a houseguest of Palmer and his wife on one occasion. After dinner that night, Mark suggested that Arnold needed help and should hire him as his agent. Palmer politely rebuffed the offer.

Later that night, Palmer showed McCormack his desk, which was overflowing with unanswered fan mail, charitable appearance requests and endorsement opportunities. As the story goes, McCormack could tell that Palmer was overwhelmed with the daunting task of going through all of this material. After Palmer and his wife had turned in for the night, McCormack stayed up and sorted through Palmer's stack of mail, sifting out the opportunities and organizing everything in a neat and orderly fashion. The next morning when Palmer walked into his den and noticed with amazement how tidy his desk was, McCormack said, "This is what I can do for you. Free you up to do what you do best."

That said, let's set the stage for what I consider to be an ideal selling scenario.

The Promise Statement

You've booked a time to meet with a prospect and sent your confirmation package. The client arrives. At the beginning of the meeting, after a few pleasantries, it's essential that you make the prospect receptive by putting him or her at ease and eliminating any skepticism. You start: "Right up front, I know your time is valuable and I know you could be doing a lot of other things right now instead of meeting with me, so I don't take that lightly. I want you to hold me accountable that this meeting will be a good use of your time.

"Also, just so you know how I work, I'm not here to sell you. My job is to analyze your current financial plan and your needs. After our meeting, I will put together a proposal outlining my observations and suggestions. We can get together in a week or so, and after reviewing the proposal you can make an informed go or no-go decision. Is that fair?"

The question *"Is that fair?"* is important because it creates an episode in the client's mind, asking him or her to envision making a decision.

Questions are the Answer

Remember Dale Carnegie's advice in his all time best-selling book *How to Win Friends and Influence People*, where he suggests that everyone's favorite topic is themselves? Ask questions and encourage the prospect to talk about things of interest and significant people in his or her life. Cover hobbies, family, and work. Let your prospect build momentum.

Most people like to talk about themselves, and if you encourage them to do so, you'll be more persuasive than ever. Your goal is to make them feel good about themselves and their potential. Prospects ultimately buy outcomes that a product, service or relationship will provide them and how it will make them feel, not just the product, service or relationship itself.

There's a Saturn car commercial on TV that uses this technique. A woman calls up the dealer to arrange a special viewing of one of their cars. When the woman appears at the dealership with her husband, he looks inside one of the cars only to find a baby car seat there. The implication is that the woman had earlier found out she was pregnant and wanted to surprise her husband with the help of the dealer. It transformed buying a car into an emotional relationship.

Influence In Action

When it comes to asking questions of your prospects, a good reminder is the acronym ACE. Ask people for their *advice* or opinion. Pay people a sincere *compliment*. And invite people to *express* themselves. You can also use the W5 approach that journalists use to uncover details. As the conversation unfolds, think *who, what, when, where, why* (and *how*). These words will serve to trigger new questions.

In keeping with the fact that people are naturally suspicious, buffer your questions in order to entice the person to open up. Buffer statements include:

- "Just out of curiosity, when…?"
- "If you don't mind me asking, where…?" "
- "Tell me if you would, what are…?"

Here are a couple of great questions, or styles of questions, that advisors can use with considerable success:

- I've always been interested in architecture. How did you come to choose that as your career?"

- "It sounds like you have a great family. If you don't mind me asking, what is your secret to keeping things balanced?"

- "It sounds like you're an authority on fly fishing. Tell me if you would, is it really worth flying north to one of those camps, or could you get the same results staying near the city?"

- "Your company sounds fascinating. If you don't mind me asking, are you still having fun?"

- "It's obvious you are a serious student of the financial world. Just out of curiosity, what criteria did you use to select your current financial advisor?"

- "As a financial advisor, I always like to know what my clients expect from me. Tell me, what will have to happen over the course of the next five years for you to feel that you've had a rewarding relationship?"

- "You seem like a wealthy guy. Did you bring your cheque book?" (Kidding!)

Select assumptive questions which intimate that it's pretty much a given that your prospects will want to work with you.

Before you move on, occasionally ask for embellishment to a short answer. "How do you mean?", or "Oh?", "Wow", "Is that right?" and pause. When you ask to be further enlightened, the prospect's relationship tension decreases and his or her decision-making confidence increases. That explains why it's always more powerful to resist talking and to follow up a question with another.

It is essential that you give this approach a chance to gather momentum. Let each conversation unfold at the client's pace. Stay engaged in the conversation, focusing on the prospect's responses, and don't allow yourself to drift. Resist the temptation to take over the conversation by finishing sentences, even when the prospect has stopped in mid-sentence to gather his or her thoughts. There's an old English saying that goes, "Don't talk unless you can improve the silence." Pick your spots based on the hot buttons you reveal and adjust your approach accordingly.

A classic example of this approach is illustrated in the following anecdote. An advisor was meeting with a high-power business owner to discuss the latter's insurance and tax situation. The advisor found the prospect to be a little on edge, so he just sat back and listened to him.

After a while, the advisor discovered that the prospect had just sold a majority position in his business for a great deal of money, but he was experiencing some remorse because he had given up control of his company. The money he had realized couldn't replace the sense of purpose that came with being the sole decision-maker. The advisor decided to form his presentation around one key benefit: that if the prospect were to die, in addition to leaving a great sum of money and taking advantage of tax opportunities, he would essentially still be in control of his family's financial future. It was one of the advisor's most rewarding transactions – financially and professionally.

Another aspect of your approach that will encourage the prospect to open up is to radiate friendliness. As the old Jewish saying goes, "Don't open a store unless you know how to smile."

Good questions help you avoid feature dumping and so too does the following simple technique. It is called the "feature/benefit/what this means to you" formula. Simply put, you introduce the prospect to a feature that you know is relevant to his or her situation. You follow by explaining the benefit of the feature. You then put the prospect into the situation by telling them precisely how that benefit will affect them. As a simple example, I'll use the formula in the following little mini-script, which discusses the benefits of disability insurance:

- "Many people feel their biggest asset is their home. So they insure it. But realistically, their biggest asset is their ability to make money. Some people are so used to making money easily that they tend to take it for granted over time. Which explains why most people "live up to their income," meaning they would find it tough to miss just a few paycheques. Disability insurance provides the confidence in knowing that should you ever be unable to perform the duties of your job, you'll still realize an income. What this ultimately means to you is that by insuring your greatest asset, you won't have to worry about losing some of your other assets. When it comes to something this important, it really is better to have it and not need it than to need it and not have it. Does that make sense?"

The Contrast Principle

When presenting certain products, it's always a good idea to present two options to the prospect rather than just one. With one option, it's either yes or no. With two options, it's either yes or yes.

A good technique that capitalizes on contrast is the *high-low* technique. For example, a computer store advertises a computer package for $2799 and right beside it is another package for $4995. The store is hoping that you'll say to yourself, "That $2799 package looks like a great deal!" (Incidentally, politicians do this all the time. They'll introduce a tax increase of 7% and wait for public response. If there is an outcry, they'll adjust it down to 5% and look like heroes, even though they were prepared to offer 5% in the first place.) So present two options, and let the person select rather than commit.

As the presentation is progressing and you sense that you've created a comfortable and receptive environment, gauge your approach on such things as body language. Constrained enthusiasm and being detail-oriented is vital in order to sway an analytical, left-brain personality style. More enthusiasm and a little playful humour will better impact an open, right-brain personality style.

Regardless of the style you use, it's important to probe occasionally with a subtle *trial close* to see how well the prospect has connected with you.

My favourite trial close showed up in the aforementioned mini-script about disability insurance: "Does that make sense?" It might not seem like much, but a few questions such as these sprinkled throughout your presentation might be enough to put a prospect into a more confident state of mind.

This technique, incidentally, stems from what is called an *ascending close*, and it was developed in, of all sectors, the encyclopaedia business. The premise was that if you could get the prospect to say "yes" to several non-threatening questions, he or she would feel that much more confident when the big 'yes' question was presented. Here's how it worked: A door-to-door salesman would walk up to the house, knock on the door and ask, "Do you live here?" to which the person would say "yes." The salesman would then say, "Do you believe in top quality education for your children?"

And so it would go. It sounds pretty silly, but when it comes down to human nature, "yes" momentum is a powerful thing. So be sure to trial-close casually yet methodically throughout the conversation. Of course, if you get an affirmative, "Yes, sounds good to me, let's go with it," don't put the prospect off. Don't say, "Well hold on, I'm not quite done my presentation, let's cover some more details." WRITE IT UP!

Here's another good trial-close: "Is that consistent with your investment philosophy?"

Quality #5: Negotiating

If you've done a good job in the presentation phase, you'll have uncovered and addressed most objections that the client has. Of course, even with a solid approach and with terrific trial closes, you'll still occasionally face some resistance. Or the prospect will simply stall. In these situations, you have to use negotiating tactics that will help the prospect deal with you on mutually beneficial terms.

Personally, I love the process of negotiating. Whether I'm the buyer or the vendor, I'm always trying to improve my situation. My favourite technique when I'm buying something is to flinch when the vendor gives me his or her price. If, for example, I'm checking into a hotel, I'll ask for the corporate rate. When I'm given a price, I pause and then ask, "Is that the best you can do?" More often than not, I'll get a better deal. And that technique works in virtually every negotiating situation imaginable (except at tax time, of course, but I'm working on it).

I kind of liken the negotiating process to tennis. When you're standing in your court, you serve to your opponent's court to see if they can return the ball. Don't read me wrong. I'm not cheap, and I'm not trying to swindle someone for a lower price. I want to pay what's fair; that's the essence of capitalism. The vendor is looking out for himself; so too is the buyer. It's whatever the market will bear. If you've ever been to Hong Kong or Manila, you know exactly what I mean.

My point is this: when someone resists your promotion, don't hold it against that person. Smile to yourself and think, "Let the games begin."

Objections can come in a variety of situations. Indecision about taking action, not wanting to give you all of their assets, and paying fees are among the most common.

One of the first things you have to consider is the prospect's spouse and bringing that person onside. Before you voice any objections, let me tell you why. If you alienate the spouse, you are looking at an unproductive outcome. It's a fact of life. As my wife says, I'm the rooster, but she runs the roost.

Along those lines, beware of the good-cop/bad-cop roles that spouses often play. (It's a situation similar to one in which you'd find two corporate decision-makers.) Don't get roped in or flustered when this occurs; respond professionally and respectfully until the charade fizzles out on its own, which it usually does.

Take The High Road

An essential element to remember when negotiating with prospective clients is to be respectful of their opinions and not be confrontational. When you are faced with what is essentially the job of telling someone he or she is wrong, be diplomatic in order to help that person see both sides of the equation.

If, for example, a prospect is not embracing your fee philosophy and in turn tells you what his or her terms of engagement are, a good response might be, "While that is a good approach, this is far too important for you not to consider your options and draw an informed comparison, don't you think?"

For emphatic objections, it might go beyond a negotiating issue – it could be a philosophical difference. When these situations occur, I highly recommend you take a stand and use what is called the *take-back* approach. Basically, you back away from the prospect to see where that person really stands. You can say, "I have to tell you that my approach is not for everyone because I'm not very flexible in the way I do things. In order to make informed decisions, I need to manage all of my clients' assets, and I insist on using a time-tested approach. My investment philosophy is not on trial. It is proven and is being used by some of the world's most successful investors.

"If you're looking for an advisor who will flip-flop from concept to concept, always chasing last year's top return generators, I'm not your guy. If you're looking for an advisor with frankly a boring yet methodical approach, then I'm the advisor for you."

And then wait. Don't say a word. One of two things will happen. The prospect will ask, "Well, what do you mean?" or say, "Well, I guess we won't be doing business together." Either response should be music to your ears.

However, if you're talking with a prospect who you really want to bring onside yet still find resistant, you have to get creative in order to achieve acquiescence. First, determine if the prospect is simply stalling. For example, when a prospect sometimes challenges you on paying fees, if you say, "Let's come back to that," you might find that it wasn't such a big deal for that person after all.

However, if it is something that is obviously an important issue to the prospect, you might have to be firmer:

- "Fees are a surprise to some investors who are not used to paying them. When it comes right down to it, everything costs more than people expect, but cost is really only an issue if there is no return. In other words, it's not what something costs – it's what it is *worth* that really counts."

Or you can be more direct with arguments that your fees are too much:

- "As compared to what?"

Put the ball back in their court so that they will expand for you.

Or you could say:

- "Discounters are illegal!" (I'm just kidding.)

A Little Shakespeare Never Hurt

Sometimes embellishments are appropriate. For example: "Up until a few years ago, my type of service was only available for top-level investors. The up and comers were forced to be transaction-oriented, while high-calibre investors had a dedicated specialist working for them who truly had a vested interest in their futures rather than in making commissions." Then tell the Picasso painting anecdote.

It also reminds me of the story of the plumber, as silly as it sounds. A plumber was called upon to discover why a pipe was rattling every time a tap was turned on. Within a couple of minutes, he had found the problem. He took out his hammer and tapped the pipe. Sure enough, the rattling stopped. He then took out his invoice book and charged the homeowner five dollars for tapping the pipe and twenty dollars for knowing where to tap.

A freeway costs you nothing, but it is often congested and not in very good shape. A toll road costs you a little, but it's usually smooth sailing, and you get to your destination faster and with less stress.

If you find yourself in a situation where you are going to make a concession in order to solidify the transaction, allow me to give you a few thoughts. First, always be willing to walk away from a sale. While I'm no different than the next person in wanting to close every sale I engage in, at what cost? I don't mean to sound elitist, but I have walked away from a couple of meaningful sales simply because I knew the commission wasn't going to compensate for the difficult personality of the buyer. As a result, I felt empowered. True, I could have used the money. But today, if I find myself negotiating with someone I'm not getting along with, I feel good just in knowing that I don't have to take the deal. And I'm certain I transmit a different air to that person. The pop psychology spin on this scenario is that sometimes people try harder to get something that's eluding them, and they push away that which is easily attained.

Be certain to ask questions which will reveal any misrepresentations about alleged competitors' claims, semantics, the opinions of so-called experts and so on. If a prospect is leaning on you, don't give in right away. Tell him, "I really think we would work well together, but I just can't bend on this. If I could, I would…"

The Big Push

If you still are willing to bend, make all of your concessions conditional. If you are going to lower a fee or remove even the smallest hurdle on which a client is stuck, make the client work for it. Here is what I mean:

First, before you announce your intention and commit yourself, verify the prospect's commitment to you. You might say, "As I understand it, you're telling me that if I waive this small fee, you'll transfer all of your assets to me and allow me to quote on your office group plan?" Get the prospect to confirm his or her intentions.

- "[Mr. Prospect], I really want to work with you. I know I can learn a lot from you, and I'm certain that we'll develop a great relationship. I'm not normally one to stray from my business approach. However, I really do want to work with you. I'll tell you what I'm willing to do. Undoubtedly, you associate with a lot of good people. I'm prepared to forego this fee on your retirement plan if you will introduce me to at least one of your business associates, provided, of course, that I deliver great service and have earned the right. Is that fair?"

For a prospect who is resistant in giving you all of her assets, but who promises long-term potential and is willing to concede a piece of her portfolio, you might say:

- "I would not normally consider doing this; however, I really do feel we'll work well together. If I manage what you have well, if you feel I'm bringing you more value than your other advisor, and if you feel I've earned the right, in twelve months I am going to insist that you move everything to me. If I don't exceed your expectations, then we'll keep the status quo. Is that fair?"

If the prospect doesn't respond favourably or if you find the prospect vacillating, ask a direct question:

- "Tell me, if you would, what would have to happen for us to close this transaction while we are here together?"

Still no go? Sometimes the real issue is two or three questions deep. Keep digging. Press for the truth, if you dare:

- "Is this (issue) really what's standing in the way of us doing business, or is there something else? Is it me or something I've said that's turned you off?"

Generally, this will soften people. If you want this person to become a client, lean respectfully to uncover the truth.

While I love negotiating, a good negotiator is one who can preempt and uncover unspoken objections so that the conversation never becomes confrontational. Hopefully, these tips will be helpful as tools of last resort.

Quality #6: Presenting

The ability to present persuasively to a group of people is an essential quality for everyone in business. Whether you are invited to speak at a Chamber of Commerce breakfast, a Young Entrepreneurs luncheon or a client dinner, your perception in the marketplace will increase considerably if you can speak effectively. The following little anecdote underscores my point: In ancient Greece, when Aschenes spoke, the crowd said, "What a speech!" But when Demosthenes spoke, the crowd roared, "Let us march!"

Here are a couple of pointers on making presentations (sad to say, I tried to fit in another acronym, but the editor has seen more than enough):

- *Study your audience.* It sounds trite but I'll say it anyway: be prepared. Get to know something about your audience and the organization to which you're speaking.

One advisor researched the history of the Chamber of Commerce before he spoke. He was so thorough that when the president got up to thank him, he asked if he could profile the advisor in the chamber's next newsletter.

Before I left to do my first seminars in England, I bought several British newspapers and business magazines to familiarize myself with the nuances of the marketplace. It bolstered my confidence immensely.

Our office worked with an advisor who held a seminar for high school students, many of whom were children of clients. It was incumbent that we create a seminar that would be a "me too" for a teenager. This was no easy task. Fortunately, I had recently listened to an audiocassette featuring Peter Lynch called *Learn to Earn*. Lynch used a great analogy about two young people, one who bought a new Camaro and another who bought a used car for considerably less money and invested the rest. We modified the example a little but basically the theme was, "You can be cool, driving a car that will very quickly depreciate, cost more in insurance and end up being a used car itself sooner rather than later. Forty percent of the cost of a new car is artificial because it goes toward advertising and commissions. Who is more cool, someone with an overpriced car or someone with a big fat bank account?"

The advisor described which companies to avoid when investing and which to consider. He used props, like a can of Coca-Cola, Johnson & Johnson skin care products and products from other blue chip companies that the students could place. He told the story about a hockey player who had signed to a big contract with the Colorado Avalanche Hockey Team. The only reason the team could afford to sign this player was because the company also owned the movie production division that had released the hugely successful film *Air Force One* starring Harrison Ford. The advisor told the students, "While the company seems pretty glamorous on the surface, do you really want to invest in a business that is unsure about where their money is going to come from? Own stocks in companies whose success is virtually a sure thing. He finished with a story about saving for a rainy day; he asked the kids to adopt the Ant Theory. He told them that ants work hard all summer, storing food because they know that winter is just around the corner. The kids loved his seminar.

- *Have a script.* Part of being prepared is having a script. Again, as with selling, I'm not suggesting you become a rigid, wooden speaker. You have to be spontaneous. On the other hand, you can't wing it. Public speaking is interesting in that, when you stand up to speak, your mind often sits back down. I've gone blank several times. Thankfully, my scripted presentation got me back on track quickly.

- *Have Flow.* There is a simple rule in presenting: Connect with the audience early, be brief and finish strong.

Humour is a good way to connect with a group early on. It warms people up and puts them at ease. But don't tell a joke with a punch line as it can backfire. If it isn't well received, people know it bombed. The key is to say something funny. One speaker I saw on a cold January day started off after the introductory applause subsided by saying, "Did you hear what the cow said to the farmer on the cold winter morning? Thanks for the warm hand." It took a second, but the audience laughed at this silly icebreaker.

Another advisor who was doing what is normally a dry seminar on tax planning added a couple of humorous points. "We live in a great country," he said, "and as such, we have to pay our fair share of taxes. But you don't want to pay more than your share. There is a difference between tax evasion and tax avoidance. I think it's about seven years." He also made this point about the media: "Take what the media has to say about the economy with the proverbial grain of salt. The media have accurately forecasted seventeen of the last three recessions."

To connect further, after your opening pleasantries, ask a question that will ensure everyone's response. I know one advisor who starts his speeches by saying, "Let me ask all of you a question. How many of you would like to learn the secrets of successful investing used by the greatest investors from around the world?" I know it's simple, but they put up their hands. Getting people involved is critical.

Another rule in speaking is to leave them wanting more. Brevity is important because it has been proven that the average attention span is about fifteen minutes long. Unless you're a phenomenal speaker, people start to squirm and daydream if you go any longer. Don't dump the whole load on people; leave them wanting more and give them a reason to want to meet with you individually after your presentation.

If you want to finish strong, I recommend you end your speech by linking it to something you said at the beginning and by stirring audience emotions and enthusiasm with a challenge or promise statement. The advisor who asks the question about the secrets of the world's greatest investors wraps up his speeches like this: "Wouldn't it be great to go to bed every night knowing that your financial plan is sound? Wouldn't it be great to teach your kids time-tested principles for financial independence? Wouldn't it be great to go to work only because you want to? By using the strategies of the best, all of that and more can become a reality for all of us."

- *Study the Art.* Several good books have been written on the subject, including Peter Urs Bender's best seller *Secrets of Power Presentations* and *"I Can See You Naked"* by Ron Hoff. As good as books are, though, the best way to realize a quantum leap in your presentation skills is to record yourself and review the tape. A step further would be to send the tape to a speaking coach. If you want feedback, make it either your own or that of a coach. Whatever you do, do not fish for feedback from attendees. Let them volunteer. If you did a good job, they'll tell you. If you did an average job, they will still tell you so, but their enthusiasm might be guarded. The worst thing a speaker can do is become a victim of the Approval Syndrome.

As you study, you become more confident and as such will conduct a better seminar. Back when we were promoting seminars, the extent of my speaking involved introducing the speakers. I was poorly prepared, both in terms of skill and from not operating with a rehearsed script. Then one day, after brutally botching an introduction, I passed the speaker as he approached the stage, and I actually apologized for doing such a bad job. He jokingly said, "Don't worry. No one was really listening." It was funny, but it got my attention. I vowed to do everything in my power from that day forward to ensure that I never embarrassed myself again (which I now realize was a pretty lofty goal).

Quality #7: Powering-up Your Magnet

Although I've saved it for last, if you had to rank all seven qualities in importance, this last one would have to top the list. Why? Because all of the other qualities are a by-product of this one. Some of the best advice I've ever received is that income rarely exceeds self-development. Back when we were promoting Jim Rohn's two-day Leadership seminar, Jim continually drove home the point that all the skills one needs to develop are learned skills. From presenting to persuading, everything can be learned and refined over time. It's not as though you were born with a 'presentation' chromosome or gene; it is a skill you craft.

I challenge all my clients to become serious students. Every book and tape you need to ensure *your* better future has already been written. I'm not just talking about books related to sharpening your financial acumen. As I said before, I've actually found that there is little correlation between how much someone knows about financial planning and how successful that person is. The advisors who reach the pinnacle of success in this business are serious students of the markets and marketing. Not only do they understand and rely on time-tested financial strategies, they also understand what it takes to be attractive to the marketplace and become the advisor of choice in the minds of people they meet.

During his seminars, renowned personal and business development coach Brian Tracy would advise everyone to read an hour a day. Leaders really are readers. But it needs to be a habit. As Warren Buffett says, "The chains of habit are too light to be felt until they are too heavy to be broken" (which can be said of both good and bad habits).

Personal development has to be part of your culture. I do my best to heed Tracy's "Hour-A-Day" advice, but it isn't easy. Because of my schedule, I have to balance my studies between books and tapes.

It really took on new meaning when I realized the importance of studying what you need to know *before* you need it, not after.

A few years back when I was experiencing some trying times in my business, I found myself in my office one weekend, trying to come up with a quick fix or silver bullet, if you will. I looked up to the top row of my bookcase to see an entrepreneurship program created by none other than Brian Tracy. I took it down and proceeded to spend the rest of weekend looking at it. You can imagine my shock as I went through the program to learn about issues that, had I only known of them before, could have prevented the difficulty I was experiencing. The interesting thing was that the program had been on my bookshelf for three years. I just hadn't got around to studying it.

As I have said, everything is a study, and every skill and technique you need in order to make yourself more attractive to the marketplace can be learned. For example, I met a financial advisor who, just prior to meeting me, spent five thousand dollars on a direct mail campaign that failed abysmally. So I asked him, "Approximately how many books have you ever read on direct mail?" His response? Approximately, zero. I can remember saying to him, "There might be a clue here." This guy is now a danger to himself and others and a menace to the integrity of marketing because he tells people not to use direct mail since it doesn't work. Not true, *his* didn't work. Interestingly, had he read one book on direct mail he would have realized that his approach was flawed.

The book you buy but don't read won't help much either. Some people hope that by simply holding a book, through osmosis the ideas will somehow start flowing. I'll be the first to admit that I've bought books I've never read, but I feel smarter just owning them. Seriously, however, when it comes to marketing skills, study, study, study. You don't need to read them all since there truly aren't many new ideas, only ones that are new to you. At the end of the day, marketing is pretty simple stuff.

The Quest For Success

The beauty of continual learning is that you get to constantly tinker with your approach. Remember, minor adjustments can lead to major improvements. You can keep making yourself more attractive to the marketplace by constantly refining what it is you do. In order to be perceived as the preferred advisor to an increasingly higher-calibre clientele, you have to balance and discriminately select what it is that you put into your mind. You grow your business by growing yourself. A combination of self-motivation and actual technique will ensure that you stay sharp.

I can't help but be reminded of a commercial on TV for the Soloflex Exercise Machine. It stated that the body is the only mechanism that gets stronger the harder you work it. That's not altogether true. The mind works the same way. But like your body, atrophy affects your mind as well. You are either in ascent or decline, never static. Our minds are like buckets of water that must continually be topped up or else the contents evaporate. And the wonderful difference between your mind and a bucket is that while the bucket doesn't grow when you top it up, your mind does, and its capacity increases.

Which is why I never have a problem justifying an investment in self-development. It is the cost of doing business. A book that costs thirty-five dollars could be worth hundreds of thousands if the ideas that flow out of it can be translated into results. I've also realized that it's actually easier to learn a skill than it is to make an excuse for a shortcoming.

Chronicle Your Life in Progress

One of Jim Rohn's best suggestions was to keep a journal. Back in 1992, I started putting my experiences – good, bad or somewhere in between – into my journal. It is one of the best things I've ever done. First of all, it allows me to capture my experiences on paper rather than trying to rely on my memory. This in turn allows me to invest my past into my future so that I won't repeat errors in judgment. At the end of each day, I usually take a few minutes to reflect upon it. At the end of the week, I replay the past seven days, flipping through each page. At the end of the month, I find myself investing an hour, recounting the month. And at the end of the year, I've invested as much as a day, turning the pages and putting myself back into those situations.

From a truly meaningful point of view, the most valuable item I will ever own and be able to hand down will be my collection of journals. From a humorous point of view, whenever I need a good laugh, I can look back at what was going on in my life a few years ago. When I do this, I find myself saying either, "What was I thinking!" or "I've come a long way."

Authentic Achievement

Reviewing one's thoughts and activities is an effective process when planning and setting goals. Goals are your reasons 'why' and when your reasons why are clear, the 'how' becomes clearer. I find it revealing as to what an advisor will set as his or her goals. Many people, when I first meet them, set financial goals. Right away, I remind them that it's not what they *get* that makes them valuable, it's what they *become*. How many stories of unhappy rich people does one have to hear before this sinks in? Financial goals on their own are great, but they can be hollow. What you accumulate is a good way to keep score, but the real value comes from what you accomplish. Which is the primary reason I ask my clients this question: "What kind of skills must you develop and what kind of person must you become in order to achieve your goals?" This prompts them to look closely at themselves and focus on the core issues that will ultimately lead them to their objectives. If you believe in the Law of Attraction, you know that you must make yourself more attractive to attract what it is you want.

Is It Really Lonely At The Top? The Law of Environment Revisited

I tell my clients of the importance of masterminding as it relates to their personal development. At the outset of the chapter on prospecting, I mentioned how critical the Law of Environment is to your professional – and I would go as far as to say personal – growth. Recall for a moment the Mastermind Alliance and the importance of putting yourself around good people. We are all products of the milieu in which we surround ourselves. If I associate with people who are negative and cynical, I will become a product of that environment. The problem is I won't even realize the spiraling effects. Mahatma Gandhi advised never to wrestle with a pig. And he was right in saying that you both get dirty, but the pig likes it.

So it is important that you target the best, work with the best and surround yourself with the best people you can. Surround yourself only with the builders in life. Remember to live with compassion and take note of cautionary tales. Everyone's life is either a warning or an example.

Be a serious student of business, but don't forget to fashion a good life too. I have found just as much inspiration and guidance from books by Confucius, Ayn Rand, Victor Hugo, Hugh McLennan and Taylor Caldwell as I have from any business book. I like to listen to music that gets my adrenaline pumping but also to the likes of Ottmar Liebert, which helps me to reflect. Travel has opened my eyes too.

What I've discovered is that making money has its rewards but that it's basically anticlimactic. I'll say it again: it's not what you get or accumulate that makes you valuable in life. It's what you become and achieve. Your character is where true value is found. Ayn Rand wrote, "Of all the achievements open to you, the one that makes all others possible is the creation of your own character." I am ardently convinced that the most liberating feeling stems from never-ending improvement and investing your improvements in other people, especially children. When you teach the entrepreneurial spirit to a child and inspire a boy or girl to feel optimism and confidence, you have left the ultimate profit. When you conduct five seminars for high school kids, you get to hear the seminar yourself five times. Everyone wins.

Set Yourself Free

Finally, I'd like to leave you with this little bit of advice: detach. This business can become an addiction. Get away as often as you must to keep yourself sharp. The longer I'm around something and the more familiar it is to me, the more I tend to take it for granted or lose my objectivity. It's also known as the Law of Familiarity. True, hard work is essential to success. But I have clients who take three months off every year, yet they get more done than others do who never take a holiday. Always look to nature for clues. A friend told me of something written by the ancient Chinese sage Lao-tzu who, through careful meditation and observation, stated that the state of weather is most often calm and serene. A thunderstorm, while intense and active, can't sustain itself for long. That observation was a profound insight for me about output and expending energy.

I've yet to meet a financial advisor who didn't want to take care of his or her clients. My contention is that the best way to take good care of them is to take impeccable care of yourself. There exists an old saying that goes, "I'll take care of me for you." You can't say it any better than that.

Treat yourself as your own best client. Look out for yourself and savour your achievements. Treat your company as a client, not an employer. You are an entrepreneur and the only actions you can control are your own.

Earn your rest, but make it a necessity, not an objective. Remember the adage that says a lazy man doesn't know when he resting. Reward yourself and come back better than ever. If you love what you do, take the necessary steps to keep it that way for the rest of your life. It could be the best investment you ever make.

Suggested Reading

Suggested Reading

Non-Fiction

Bender, Peter Urs. *Secrets of Power Presentations.* Toronto: The Achievement Group, 1991.

Confucius. *The Analects of Confucius (translated by Arthur Waley).* New York: Vintage Books, 1989.

Durant, Will and Ariel. *The Lessons of History.* New York: Simon and Shuster, 1968.

Frankl, Viktor E. *Man's Search For Meaning.* Pocket Books, 1988.

Galbraith, John Kenneth. *A Short History of Financial Euphoria.* New York: Viking Penguin, 1993.

Gerber, Michael E. *The E-Myth.* U.S.A.: HarperBusiness, 1986.

Graham, Benjamin. *The Intelligent Investor: A Book of Practical Counsel.* HarperCollins, 1997.

Grove, Andy. *Only The Paranoid Survive.* Doubleday, 1996.

Hill, Napoleon. *Think and Grow Rich.* Fawcett Books, 1990.

Hobson, Alan and Clarke, Jamie *The Power of Passion.*

Hoff, Ron. *"I Can See You Naked": A Fearless Guide to Making Great Presentations.* Kansas City: Andrews and McMeel, 1988.

Lewis, Herschell Gordon. *Sales Letters That Sizzle.* Lincolnwood, Ill: NTC Business Books, 1995.

Lowe, Janet. *Warren Buffett Speaks.* New York: John Wiley & Sons, Inc., 1997.

Mackay, Harvey. *Swim With The Sharks Without Being Eaten Alive.* New York: William Morrow & Company, Inc., 1988.

McCormack, Mark H. *What They Don't Teach You At Harvard Business School,* New York: Bantam Books, 1984.

Murray, Nick. *The Excellent Investment Advisor.* The Nick Murray Company, Inc., 1996.

Ogilvy, David. *Ogilvy on Advertising.* Toronto, John Wiley & Sons Canada Ltd., 1983.

O'Shaugnessy, James. *How To Retire Rich.* New York: Broadway Books, 1998.

Peters, Tom. *The Pursuit of WOW!* New York: Vintage Books, 1994.

Rohn, Jim. *Seven Strategies For Wealth and Happiness.* Rocklin, CA: Prima Publishing & Communications, 1986.

Soros, George. *Soros on Soros: Staying Ahead of the Curve.* John Wiley & Sons, 1995.

Senge, Peter. *The Fifth Discipline.* Doubleday, 1994.

Stanley, Thomas J., Ph.D. *Selling To The Affluent.* New York: McGraw-Hill, 1991.

Stanley, Thomas J., Ph. *Marketing To The Affluent.* New York: McGraw-Hill, 1988.

Stanley, Thomas T., Danko, William D., Ph.D. *The Millionaire Next Door.* Atlanta: Longstreet Press, 1996.

Tracy, Brian. *Maximum Achievement.* Fireside, 1995.

Ziglar, Zig. *See You At The Top.* Gretna, LA: Pelican Publishing Company, 1975.

Fiction
Caldwell, Taylor. *A Pillar of Iron.*

Rand, Ayn. *Atlas Shrugged.* New York, Dutton, 1957.

Rand, Ayn. *The Fountainhead (50th Anniversary edition).* Signet, 1996.

> For a more extensive listing of books,
> including an overview of content,
> check our website at
> www.dma-inbound.com

SUCCESS SOURCE RESOURCE CENTRE

THE PROMISE OF THE FUTURE $30.00

Quantity Discounts are available as follows:

10 to 24	$ 25
25 to 99	$ 20
100 +	$ 15

INBOUND QUARTERLY MARKETING REPORT $149.00

1 Year Subscription
The DMA office is a lightning rod for marketing ideas. Working with our clients, we see firsthand what works well, what to avoid, and we publish our findings. Every quarter for one year, you can have the best of the best marketing ideas delivered right to your home or office to ensure that you are on track and enjoying the path of least resistance. Subscription includes 4 printed reports packed with ideas on prospecting, promotional partnering, client marketing, personal development and much more.

SPECIAL BONUS - As a subscriber, you will also receive a special "year in review" audio cassette.

TURNKEY MARKETING SYSTEM $495.00

Several years in the making, and newly revised and updated, this popular system contains everything you need to build a marketing plan consisting of time-tested marketing strategies. Included in the system are:

✓ Dozens of ready-to-use letters, questionnaires, and other exhibits
✓ Abridged audio cassettes of *The Promise of the Future*
✓ Easy-to-use diskette containing all exhibits
✓ Impressive storage binder and bonus book

SPECIAL BONUS - One year subscription to *InBound Quarterly Marketing Report*—a $149 value.

SUCCESS SOURCE
INTERNATIONAL

(a division of Duncan MacPherson & Associates, Inc.)
431 Gilmour Street, Third Floor, Ottawa, Ontario, Canada K2P 0R5
Tel: (613) 593-8943   Fax: (613) 593-8999
E-mail: inbound@cyberus.ca   Website: www.dma-inbound.com

ORDER INFORMATION:

Name

Company

Address

City   Prov   PC

Tel

Fax

E-mail

SUCCESS SOURCE ORDER FORM

SUCCESS SOURCE
INTERNATIONAL
A DIVISION OF
DUNCAN MACPHERSON & ASSOC. INC.

FAX THIS ORDER TO:
Fax (613) 593-8999
Any questions?
Call (613) 593-8943

SHIP TO ADDRESS (If different than above)

Name

Company

Address

City   Prov   PC

VISIT OUR WEBSITE

Want more information about these and other powerful marketing products and services? It's all here:

www.dma-inbound.com
or e-mail us at:
inbound@cyberus.ca

ITEM	QTY	DESCRIPTION	SHIPPING/UNIT	PRICE	TOTAL
PF981		**The Promise of the Future** by Duncan MacPherson	$ 5.00	$ 30.00	
QMR4		**Quarterly Marketing Report** includes bonus cassette	$ 6.00	$ 149.00	
TMS2		**Turnkey Marketing System** by Duncan MacPherson & Assoc.	$ 20.00	$ 495.00	

METHOD OF PAYMENT

☐ Cheque *(make payable to Success Source International)*

☐ Mastercard   ☐ VISA   ☐ AMEX

Card #

Expiration Date

Cardholder's Name

Signature

Total Product

Shipping Charge

GST *(7% Canadian res. only)*

PST *(8% ON res. only)*

Total

Thank You!

GREAT IDEAS AND SERVICES OFFERED BY
DUNCAN MACPHERSON & ASSOCIATES INC.

GUEST SPEAKER

Duncan has become one of the most sought-after speakers in the financial services industry. From a 60-minute keynote speech at a national sales conference to a full-day intensive marketing seminar, Duncan will empower rookie and established advisors on how to unlock their marketing potential.

COACHING SERVICES

Top achievers in any field of endeavour will use a coach to help them tap into their full potential. Hire Duncan and his staff on a one-year retainer and they will:

- *Conduct an analysis of your marketing assets and establish your unique selling proposition.*
- *Create a personalized marketing plan based on your unique situation*
- *Work with you and your team throughout the year as your plan gathers momentum.*

As a special bonus, consulting clients can attend two mastermind sessions each year. These sessions allow advisors to network with other top advisors from across the continent. Clients will also receive *The Turnkey Marketing System* and a one year subscription to *InBound*.

CONFERENCE CALLS

Wouldn't it be great to have Duncan consult with your team once a quarter or even once a month? Duncan will conduct a customized phone presentation and then provide a question and answer session. This popular service is ideal for a branch or your entire firm. We'll arrange everything— booking the conference call centre and notifying your team as to the date and time of the call. The call can even be recorded for follow-up purposes. A one-year program is ideal for stimulating new ideas, for serving as a sounding board and assisting with implementations.

SPEAKERS BUREAU

Podium Productions, a division of DMA, works closely with many of the world's best speakers and trainers. When you need a speaker for a client appreciation event or a prospecting seminar, or your firm requires a keynote presenter for a conference, we can steer you in the right direction. We also offer our proven seminar marketing program as a special bonus.

Contact us for more information or to receive our special services kit:

Tel: (613) 593-8943
Fax: (613) 593-8999
inbound@cyberus.ca
www.dma-inbound.com

THE DMA WEBSITE

www.dma-inbound.com

- Marketing strategies online
- Essential reading
- Speaker's Corner
- Cool Links
- Quotation Vault

Come visit us!

INBOUND QUARTERLY MARKETING REPORT

Receive your complimentary copy of our **InBound Quarterly Marketing Report** as a thank you from all of us at DMA for purchasing *The Promise of the Future.* You'll find out what really makes us tick:

- Cutting edge marketing and selling strategies
- Tips on fine-tuning your letter campaigns
- Advisor profiles
- Timely articles by guest contributors
- Personal development ideas

The *Marketing Report* series is 8-10 pages packed with strategies to make your phone ring. Call, fax or e-mail us to order your free copy today.

Tel: (613) 593-8943
Fax: (613) 593-8999
inbound@cyberus.ca